developmental and cognitive aspects of learning to spell:

A Reflection of Word Knowledge

edited by

Edmund H. Henderson
University of Virginia
  and
James W. Beers
The College of William and Mary

INTERNATIONAL READING ASSOCIATION
800 Barksdale Road   Newark, Delaware 19711

i

Copyright 1980 by the
International Reading Association, Inc.

Library of Congress Cataloging in Publication Data

Main entry under title:
Developmental and cognitive aspects of learning to spell.

Includes bibliographies.
1. English language—Orthography and spelling—Study and teaching—Addresses, essays, lectures.
2. Spelling ability—Addresses, essays, lectures.
3. Reading (Elementary)—Addresses, essays, lectures.
I. Henderson, Edmund H. II. Beers, James W., 1946-
LB1574.D48   372.6'32   80-36699
ISBN 0-87207-941-4

Contents

Foreword

This volume on spelling is a unique contribution to IRA's list of publications. The articles by Henderson, Beers, and their colleagues are based on a well developed theoretical base. This theory, which is clearly articulated by Henderson, is the foundation for an impressive series of studies which test the theory with children of different ages and under varying conditions.

It is also impressive that the theory and research integrates a child's development of spelling ability with reading, oral language, and cognitive development. Too often those who study a particular language behavior fail to describe and discuss the interrelationships of all language behaviors. Not so with this series of articles.

Perhaps most importantly, this volume proceeds from theory to research to teaching practice. While the emphasis of the volume is on theory and research, the authors consistently emphasize teaching principles and generalizations that can guide spelling instruction. These teaching generalizations and principles may not be readily accepted by some teachers or researchers; but the authors' case is well documented throughout the volume. It is quite probable that the volume will serve as an impetus for further research, for better articulation of the components of language development, and for more theory/research-based debates about teaching spelling.

Perhaps the authors' most precise statement regarding the teaching of any language skill is stated by Edmund

Henderson in the chapter entitled "Word Knowledge and Reading Disability." He states:

> What is needed for learning to read is support in natural language, abundant reading and writing and a guided opportunity to differentiate that most remarkable of all graphic events, the written word.

The theory and research presented in this volume supports Henderson's statement and is a welcome addition to IRA's professional publications.

Roger Farr, President
International Reading Association
1979-1980

Chapter One

Developmental Concepts of Word

Edmund H. Henderson
University of Virginia

For at least the past hundred years in America the central argument between reading methodologists has been whether to teach words as wholes or words by their constituent letter parts. In each camp, there has been considerable variation on a basic theme. Some said to teach letter names; others, to teach the sounds and relate these to the letters; while still others proposed new alphabets so that letters and sounds would agree consistently. On the other side, it was argued that words should be taught, with reading following directly after. To this approach, many added an analytic program of word analysis. This so-called combination method has been the most widely used approach of all. Finally, there was Bloomfield's linguistically influenced method in which he advocated that "regular" syllable patterns be memorized by having the pupil name each letter as the unit was spoken as a whole.

Curiously, all of these approaches can be found to share a common set of assumptions about how children learn to read. First, there is the implicit assumption that children come to the task with a blank slate—that words by one device or another, must be put into their heads. Second, each approach assumes the validity of the unit selected for teaching and third, each approach assumes that such learning proceeds linearly by associative pairings that bond the spoken units to their graphic representatives.

For the past ten years, my students and I have investigated these assumptions, and we have found them wanting. We began by asking, not what *we* knew about words but, instead, what children knew about them at different stages of development and degrees of experience with written language. We have found that children do not come to school with a blank slate. To the contrary, they have learned many complex and quite wonderful things about written language before they begin to learn to read. Moreover, we believe that they must have done so if reading is to occur at all. We have found further that children advance in their knowledge of words through discernible conceptual stages and that these stages hold with great stability across different methods of instruction, mixtures of dialect, and even different languages. In short, we have found an advancing concept of word that appears to be universal for users of alphabetic language.

We contend that an understanding of what children know about words is crucial for effective instruction in reading and writing. Children do, of course, learn letters and words directly from exposure to written language. But what they can learn—indeed, even what they can *see* on the page—depends upon the conceptual frame they bring to the task. Where instruction is paced to the child's underlying conceptual grasp, almost any methodology is likely to succeed. Where this state of mind is violated or overreached, almost any method is likely to fail and lead to difficulty.

Successful teachers over the ages have been intuitively aware of these conditions. The literature is clear in showing that teacher variable is more influential than is method. The contribution our work has made is that we can now describe these stages explicitly. Thus, we can provide concrete guidance for teachers about when and how far to drive home the particular tasks they choose.

We also have found that an understanding of the conceptual aspect of word knowledge provides a new avenue for basic reading instruction. This consists of activities designed to exercise and extend children's concept of word. The tasks we have developed are modeled after a typical concept development design (8). They require children to attend to likenesses and differences among words and to form and differentiate the categories that may be discerned among the diversity of words available to them at any stage of their knowledge. The object of such study is not simply to learn rules of regularity, though these may have some temporary value. Instead, our object is to exercise and reinforce a "habit of search" which we think is absolutely necessary for an orthographic mastery of a full adult vocabulary. On the surface, these activities appear very similar to those common to many analytic phonics programs. They are, however, different from other approaches, both in management and objective. Where they have been applied in clinic and classroom, we have found them to be effective.

A Preview of the Monograph

In this introductory chapter, I will present a brief history of our research, declare our rationale, and sketch the stages of word concept we have found. Before proceeding, it may be helpful to preview the monograph as a whole. Each article has been written by a former doctoral student and, except for the theoretical paper, each is arrayed in the order in which the studies were completed. In this way, we hope the reader may get a feel for the way in which the research unfolded.

Templeton's theoretical discussion in the following chapter is technical and necessarily places a fairly heavy demand upon the reader. The chapter was included, nevertheless, because this research is relatively new, and it is important for the reader to know that this theoretical base has been examined carefully. In addition, it is hoped that the discussion might prove helpful to readers who wish to further explore this line of study.

Beers, coeditor of this volume, pioneered our early efforts to understand the linguistic theory that underlies Read's important work. In Chapter Three, Beers presents some of these background ideas and also covers an early exploratory study which we conducted jointly, his own dissertation, and several studies following from that.

Zutell and C. Beers (Chapters Five and Six) extend this initial work to other grade levels and examine the stages of word concept in relation to stages of cognitive development as defined by a selection of Piagetian tasks. Stever's article

(Chapter Four) reports her study of the effects of dialect upon the children's concepts of words. Next in the sequence, Templeton's research article reports his application of the method to children in grades six, eight, and ten. Finally, we have included a recent study by Morris (Chapter Eight) which deals with children's initial concept of word as a bound figure or object.

In presenting this series of closely related works, we have faced some fairly difficult editorial problems. Writers have written with their own voices; therefore, readers are bound to encounter stylistic differences from chapter to chapter. In addition, each study leans on a common background; thus some repetition is inevitable. We have given our best effort to keep this to a minimum. Finally, because this is research which involves some relatively new and technical terms, we have tried our best to define these as we wrote, and to avoid technicalities whenever possible.

We who have pursued this inquiry have found it high adventure. From the first vague hunch to the finding of data, from the testing of the method in different ways to coming to understand it pedagogically, it has been exciting work. Each of us has felt now and then like Cortez on his peak viewing something new and wonderful. We want as many as will try it, to share that feeling with us. To that end we have made every effort to remove heavy statistical analyses and details of research design from the body of the text. For the interested researcher, more formal presentation may be found in the literature as referenced.

At the time these papers were first assembled we were concluding 1) a new line of study in word concept (35), 2) a major replication of the method with refinement in its coding and analysis (5), and 3) the first explorations in what has now become a series of cross-cultural assessments (9,33,34). In addition, we had reached a point of understanding where we could apply what we had learned in classrooms and in the diagnostic center of our home clinic. We decided that for this monograph, Sulzby, Gentry, Gillet, Kita, and I would undertake papers that might give some sense of the use our findings have been to us in the practical business of teaching children to read. Gillet and Kita have undertaken a firsthand account of the method in action.

The essay by Gentry and Henderson reflects the power of the method in making children's early writing diagnostically interpretable and viable as a teaching tool. Sulzby's account focuses both upon the variability of response the method allows and upon the specific techniques of word study that we believe will enrich a child's concept of word. In the concluding chapter I have tried to show, with specific cases, how our stages of word knowledge have served us in a diagnostic setting.

Beginnings of the Work

During the sixties my former professor, Russell G. Stauffer, conducted a longitudinal study of the language-experience approach as it was applied to children from grades one to six (*31*). Being his colleague at that time, I had an extended opportunity to study compositions written by first grade children. What struck me forcibly was the cleverness of their misspellings. If they did not know how to spell *built* but knew the word *Bill*, they would spell the former BILLT. Of course that is not the way English spelling works, but logically and phonetically it seemed to make good sense.

In one sample of papers, Hammond (*11*) and I found that 52 percent of the running words were spelled correctly. In addition (by our then "seat-of-the-pants" analysis), 87 percent were spelled either correctly or logically correctly. Thus, these raw beginners seemed to know as much as the famous linguistically instructed computer of Hanna, Hanna, Hodges, and Rudorf (*12*).

It was also during the sixties that new research was being conducted on children's language acquisition (*2*). Before that time, most research of this kind had proceeded descriptively, for example, by counting the words of different types that children typically uttered at different ages. In the new work, researchers focused instead on syntactical errors and undertook to infer from these a concept of language that might underlie them. A classic example of the design is the one in which children were found first to use the strong verb (*go, went, gone*) correctly and then at a later stage to begin to form the past tense incorrectly as in "Daddy goed to the store." The implication was that the child, having recently learned to use inflections (in this case *ed*), overgeneralized this plan to the strong verb form. Thus, in superficial error lay the data from which to infer the onset of an underlying concept, i.e., use of inflections.

In the late sixties I began to apply this language acquisition model to children's writing. My students and I reasoned that if we could find consistent patterns in children's misspellings, then we might infer from these the underlying concept that guided their rendering of a word in printed form. In one of our first attempts, we made a massive analysis from a carefully drawn sample of first grade children's writing. We coded each error of substitution or omission for each phoneme by position in word (14). One interesting and important thing we found was that only a small portion of the huge grid was needed. This may be interpreted to say that children's early misspellings are not random. We concluded that there must be some logic to the errors they produced. At that point, however, we did not know how to unlock the mystery. It was not until we read and taught ourselves how to understand the brilliant dissertation of Read (23) that we were able to advance. An accounting of these efforts is contained in Chapter Three by Beers.

When our investigations stood in limbo, we invited Professors Goodman, Smith, and Stauffer to view our perplexity. They were all most kind and helpful. Goodman observed correctly that we were attempting too much at once. He recommended that we proceed, as he had done with his early miscue research, by a single element at a time. Smith showed us the fallacy in a statistical analysis we were proposing and saved us many wasted hours. He also raised the question of the distinction he felt must be made between reading and spelling and sent us a copy of his chapter on the topic in his forthcoming book (29).

Smith's question deserves special notice in this account because many who see our work for the first time conclude that it is simply a study of spelling. In one important sense that is true; the raw data are spelling errors or, as Read calls them, "invented spellings." We do believe that a mature concept of word underlies a writer's ability to produce, and to spell correctly, the vast lexicon of English.

How then does our work relate to reading? Smith holds that the mature reader attains speed and fluency precisely by neglecting the redundant details of orthography and syntax.

Reasoning thus, he concludes that one does not need to spell in order to read, nor does one receive much information about how words are spelled in the act of fluent reading. I am inclined to agree with this argument as it applies to the fluent reader. In the process of *becoming* such a reader, however, very different conditions prevail.

Smith himself has declared that the information source available to the reader is threefold: semantic, syntactic, and orthographic. He has used the metaphor of "tunnel vision" to describe the dilemma of the beginning reader, whose ignorance of orthography (lack of word knowledge) leads to phonemic puzzling and thence to an information overload. So it is that the beginner limps along word by word.

In my opinion, Smith's discussion of the beginning reader is a useful one, and I agree fully that such beginners must have support (prior knowledge of the text, for example), if they are to move forward in reading and so acquire the orthographic knowledge initially wanting. However, I do not agree that reading ever becomes *independent* of word knowledge. What is vital in print is precisely what the author put there. The strong case for this point is the reading of a metaphor (22,27). Readers must first apprehend what is written and thereafter do with it what they can. If they constuct what is not there, then they have erred as readers. Only a very highly refined cognitive knowledge of words, including the relationship of these to syntax, prosody, and the grammar of style, will suffice to keep readers honest and provide them the freedom to think as they read.

Some Thoughts on Text Perception

To my knowledge, no one has yet succeeded in developing a wholly adequate theoretical model of the reading process (18). We are forced with despair and wonder to agree with Huey (16) that it really is a miracle. Nonetheless, models do abound in the contemporary literature and their influence is significant.

Most prominent among models today are those derived from information theories which employ a computer-like flow chart design. They work from the bottom up (20) or from the top down (19) or, in the case of Rumelhart (26), in both directions simultaneously. The latter seems to me the most plausible from a descriptive point of view, but none is really adequate to the task. For one thing, the brain is patently different from a computer. As Eccles (4) has observed, the brain lacks the electrical energy to drive such machinery.

To my mind, Gibson (6) has come closest to a satisfactory statement of the conditions that must be met for a working model. If I interpret her correctly, her plan is cognitively based, energy efficient, and responsive to but independent of predicative thought. The crux of the argument, as I see it, turns on the way in which we define the term *feature* as the cuing element of print.

In most computer models the information search begins as concrete graphic features are addressed. These are then processed into higher-order apprehensions at each time of fixation. This plan seems both unwieldy and unlikely. In speech perception we do not, without conscious effort, perceive raw sound (21). Instead, we unconsciously construct abstract, phonemically-segmented syllables which are sampled across the prosodic flow, making sense of it or not as we can or will. Analogous circumstance must hold, I think, in text perception. What we learn as we learn to read must be those abstract relational features that text affords. Thereafter, it is these that are sampled directly at each fixation point and sense is made or not, as it is in attending to speech. It is my belief that our studies of children's errors in spelling reflect indirectly and in part the underlying process through which the featural components of text are gradually differentiated.

Both Smith and Gibson have stated from the beginning that the features of letter, word, and text are abstract. Smith's information-theory description (28) of the "feature list," however, seems to have led many to a far more concrete conceptualization of the phenomenon than he perhaps intended. Gibson (7) has written explicitly to correct this misapprehension in regard to her own work.

In my opinion, a viable theory of reading must begin with the assumption that abstract featural components *are* the raw material of text perception. I propose that these features are learned and can be learned only by human beings. This is to say that the capacity to do so is specific to the language centers of the human brain. Finally, I propose that we can

Henderson

identify the progression toward this achievement by observing human behavior in relation to graphics developmentally.

Some Behavioral Evidence

One early event in childhood has long struck me as remarkable. When very young children are first taught to examine pictures (as when reading a cloth book, for example), they will often expect on turning a page to see the other side of the figure. Learning that graphics may represent reality is a very high level achievement. Most animals cannot do it.

Gibson (8) has charted most interestingly the stages by which children become progressively aware of letters and words and has shown how much children learn before they can actually read. Goodman (10) and her students have described in some detail children's ability to "read" pictures and signs at quite early ages. Clay (3), however, makes it unmistakably clear that reading signs and reading words in text are very different matters.

Reading, like speaking, has a temporal component. While words are spatially arrayed, that array always has a direction. Its perception takes place over time. This directional/temporal aspect is what distinguishes word and phrase identification from other kinds of seeing—be it figures in space or pictures of such figures. Text represents language.

The way children achieve this new order of seeing is an interesting one. It is well known that most who learn to read on their own do so by telling a familiar story to a book that has been read to them often (32). The special cadence of story language has the effect of slowing down the pace and highlighting word segments more clearly than is the case in common speech. Doubtless this helps the learner discern the significance of spaces and thus to find, identify, and remember individual words.

The ability to identify words in text as individual nameable objects appears to be a "watershed" event in learning to read (see Morris, Chapter Eight). Children who cannot point to individual words as they "read" a memorized text learn few words and cannot reliably segment spoken words. Children who *can* identify individual words in text learn words and are able to segment by phoneme with astonishing accuracy. It seems to me that the notorious difficulty prereaders have with tasks of auditory discrimination (8) hinges on this phenomenon. It is not that prereaders cannot discriminate phonemes or learn so called letter sounds; in fact, they must in order to speak. It is simply that, lacking a stable concept of word as a bound figure with a beginning and an end, they cannot know where to focus their attention.

Stages of Word Knowledge

The characteristics of children's spelling errors lend themselves to grouping by developmental stages. It is these that I believe reflect a progressive differentiation of orthographic knowledge which in time underlies the abstract relational features by which words are identified in text and produced in written form.

As Gibson(8) has shown, children enjoy scribbling at a very early age. Thereafter, their aimless markings evolve into precise drawings. At this time, children can be found who will accompany their pictures with a very special scribble which they will say is writing. At this point, they begin to ask about and learn to point to letters or write them.

Prereading children who know their letters will begin to write in various ways. The most common production is one in which letters, invented letters, and numbers are set down in a jumble and in any direction. Precocious children who have learned the direction their language takes may at this preliterate stage produce some astonishingly "readable" efforts spelled not by word, but by prosodic unit. Were such children German, they would be likely to spell *Lieblingskuh* (favorite cow) LIBGSKU correctly as one word but with certain letters omitted. Later, they would be likely to separate the two word-like elements, which in German are spelled as one (*15*). This new error, LIBGS KU, appears to derive from the salience of their newly discovered knowledge of word.

When children learn what words are, their spelling errors change accordingly. Among kindergarteners, Gentry (*5*) found an abrupt halt in the random directionless inventions. In their place, words were spelled by a single letter. I infer that children who do this know what a word is *not* but not what it *is* with sufficient stability to track it through in detail.

When the concept of word is firmly held, a letter-name strategy emerges. This is the pattern first discovered by Read (23) and studied next in the classroom setting by Beers and Henderson (1). At this stage, as the name implies, children spell by the phonemic feature that is emphasized in each letter as it is named in the alphabet of their language. Thus, the German children would spell *Liebling*, LIBG, while English children would spell *leaf*, LEF. This is so because in German the name of the letter *i* is pronounced like our long *e*.

I have drawn the following implications about word knowledge from the various phenomena of letter-name spelling. Clearly, children at this stage have objectified *word* as a stable object. Equally clearly they are able to discern and match letters to the phonemic elements in a consistent direction. Such an achievement is remarkable and involves a considerable level of abstraction. Conceptually, on the other hand, the letter-name stage is noticeably mechanical and concrete: word matches word; letter matches sound left to right. In addition, words so construed (see Chapters Four, Nine) are burdened by homography—many high frequency words are "to the mind's eye" spelled alike. In my judgment, this may account for the fragile competence of beginning readers. If they are pressured to acquire sight words at this stage, confusion invariably results.

Next in order (for English children at least) comes the stage we have labeled "vowel transition." Now a new brand of error occurs. Long vowels which heretofore were frankly spelled by letter name (LEF for *leaf*) are now accompanied by a marker or silent letter—often a faulty one (LEIF, LEFE, for example). Comparable errors may be found in German between the short and continuent vowels and their marker as in *mir* and *mirr*. This stage and one succeeding it are reported in Chapter Four. My inference about word knowledge at this point is this: No longer is "word" confined to concrete linear matchings of letters to sounds. Instead, patterns begin to function relationally. Thus *tion* in *ration* is pronounced *shun* and not *tie on* and the *a* in *bake* is not pronounced like the *a* in *back*. It is the relationship among the letters in each word that indicates the pronunciation. So rendered, English words are better differentiated and their underlying features become more effective as cues.

This, of course, is not the end of the affair. Syntactic, semantic, and derivational aspects of word come into play and serve in a relational manner to underpin those regularities that constitute the featural cues of text. Certain aspects of this evolving process are suggested in Templeton's study (Chapter Seven). From our exploratory work across languages (Finnish, German, French, Spanish, and Chinese), I am inclined to believe that these progressions have a marked commonality even though they are expressed in different tongues and in different writing systems.

Conclusion

My reason for writing at length in this introductory chapter has been to provide a road map for what follows. To some, our work will be altogether new. It is my hope that this retrospective overview may both forecast the studies that follow and prove itself more convincing when they have been read.

The stages of word knowledge we have found will be of interest to the serious teacher of reading and writing. They are not rigid behavioral criteria, nor do they admit the derivation of any particular method of instruction. They are, instead, very broad and human developmental events in the progress toward literacy.

As James (17) correctly said in 1892, the science of the mind's laws cannot prescribe methods directly. "Teaching is an art and must always advance through the intermediary of an inventive mind using its (own) originality." But science can set limits which define what is clearly right and clearly wrong. James put it thus:

> But, if the use of psychological principles thus be negative rather than positive, it does not follow that it may not be a great use, all the same. It certainly narrows the path for experiments and trials. We know in advance, if we are psychologists, that certain methods will be wrong, so our psychology saves us from mistakes. It makes us, moreover, more clear as to what we are about. We gain confidence in respect to any method which we are using as soon as we believe that it has theory as well as practice at its back (p. 26).

It is my belief that our stages of word knowledge, easily discerned in children's invented spellings, will provide sound guidance to teachers as they invent new methods of study for their children.

References

1. Beers, J., and E. Henderson. "First Grade Children's Developing Orthographic Concepts," *Research in the Teaching of English*, Fall 1977.
2. Brown, R. *A First Language: The Early Stages*. Cambridge, Massachusetts: Harvard University Press, 1973.
3. Clay, Marie M. "Early Childhood and Cultural Diversity in New Zealand," *Reading Teacher*, 29 (January 1976), 333-342.
4. Eccles, John C. Personal observation during his visit to the McGuffey Reading Center, February 24, 1977.
5. Gentry, J.R. "A Study of the Orthographic Strategies of Beginning Readers," doctoral dissertation, School of Education, University of Virginia, 1977.
6. Gibson, E. "Reading for Some Purpose," in James F. Kavanagh and Ignatius A. Mattingly (Eds.), *Language by Ear and by Eye*. Cambridge, Massachusetts: MIT Press, 1972.
7. Gibson, E. "How Perception Really Develops: A View from Outside the Network," in David LaBerge and S. Jay Samuels (Eds.), *Basic Processes in Reading*. Hillsdale, New Jersey: LEA Publishers, 1977.
8. Gibson, E., and H. Levin. *The Psychology of Reading*. Cambridge, Massachusetts: MIT Press, 1975.
9. Gill, Charlene. "A Study of the Orthographic Strategies of French Speaking Children," doctoral dissertation, School of Education, University of Virginia, 1979.
10. Goodman, Y. "Language Development Research and Its Impact on Curriculum and Instruction," an IRA/NCTE cosponsored series. Preconvention Institute, International Reading Association, Atlanta, Georgia, April 1979.
11. Hammond, D., and E. Henderson "An informal Analysis of Spelling Errors in the Writing of First Graders," unpublished paper, University of Delaware, 1966.
12. Hanna, P., and others. *Phoneme-Grapheme Correspondence as Cues to Spelling Improvement*. Washington D.C.: U.S. Government Printing Office, 1966.
13. Henderson, E. "The Cloth Book," unpublished manuscript.
14. Henderson, E., T. Estes, and S. Stonecash. "An Exploratory Study of Word Acquisition among First Graders at Midyear in a Language Experience Approach," *Journal of Reading Behavior*, 4 (1972), 21-30.
15. Henderson, E., and C. Temple. Research in progress, 1979.
16. Huey, Edmund B. *The Psychology and Pedagogy of Reading*. Cambridge: MIT Press, 1979.
17. James, William. *Talks to Teachers on Psychology and to Students on Some Life's Ideals*. New York: W.W. Norton, 1958.
18. Kavanagh, J., and I. Mattingly. *Language by Ear and by Eye: The Relationship between Speech and Reading*. Cambridge: MIT Press, 1972.
19. Kinch, Walter. *The Representation of Meaning in Memory*. Hillsdale, New Jersey: Lawrence Erlbaum Associates, 1974.
20. LaBerge, D., and S. Jay Samuels. "Toward a Theory of Automatic Information Processing in Reading," *Cognitive Psychology*, 6 (1972), 293-323.
21. Lieberman, P. *On the Origins of Language*. New York: Macmillan, 1975.
22. Palermo, D.S. *Psychology of Language*. Glenview, Illinois: Scott, Foresman, 1978.
23. Read, C. "Children's Perceptions of the Sounds of English: Phonology from

Three to Six," unpublished doctoral dissertation, Harvard University, 1970.
24. Read, C. "Preschool Children's Knowledge of English Phonology," *Harvard Educational Review*, 41 (February 1971), 1-34.
25. Read, C. *Children's Categorization of Speech Sounds in English.* Urbana, Illinois: NCTE, 1975.
26. Rumelhart, D.E. "Toward an Interactive Model of Reading,"in Stanslav Dornic (Ed.), *Attention and Performance.* Hillsdale, New Jersey: Lawerence Erlbaum Associates, 1977.
27. Schlagal, Robert. "On the Nature and Significance of Metaphor," unpublished manuscript, University of Virginia, 1979.
28. Smith, F. *Understanding Reading.* New York: Teachers College Press, 1979.
29. Smith, F. *Psycholinguistics and Reading.* New York: Holt, Rinehart and Winston, 1973.
30. Smith, F. *Reading without Nonsense.* New York: Teachers College Press, 1979.
31. Stauffer, R.G. *Action Research in LEA Instructional Procedures.* Newark, Delaware: University of Delaware, 1976.
32. Teale, W. "Positive Environments for Learning to Read: What Studies of Early Readers Tell Us," *Language Arts*, 55 (November/December 1978).
33. Temple, C. "Spelling Errors in Spanish," doctoral dissertation, University of Virginia, 1978.
34. Temple, C., and E. Henderson. "Spelling Errors in German," unpublished manuscript, 1979.
35. Tucker, Elizabeth Sulzby. "Children's Explanations of Word Similarities in Relation to Word Knownness," doctoral dissertation, University of Virginia, 1978.

Chapter Two

What Is a Word?

Shane Templeton
Emory University

Depending on whom you ask—linguist, psychologist, teacher, or child—words may be described as sounds, referents, meanings, groups of letters bounded on either side by white spaces, things that come out of our mouths, morphemes, linguistic devices, generalized perceptual tests, or things our mothers tell us. People have been busy for quite some time trying to determine what words are and how they work for individuals; this enterprise has been underway at least since the fourth century B. C. when the Greeks debated whether words bear a *natural* relationship to the things they represent or a *conventional* relationship in which people arbitrarily assign sounds to meanings. To simplify the Greeks' argument considerably: Is the word "tinkle" in our vocabulary because it "kind of sounds like" the sound to which it refers? This "onomatopoeic" debate is still being argued today, but there are other questions about words that are probably more important. The purpose of this discussion is to provide a working concept of what cognitive and linguistic theories suggest words are, for these conceptualizations have to explain what *children* initially think words are, what they will come to know about words, and what they can only be told we probably know. In this latter regard, there is considerably more that all of us in some sense "know" about words but will never be able to understand at a conscious level.

Two Faces of the Knowledge Coin

Perhaps the most fascinating knowledge that resides within our brains is that knowledge we cannot get at introspectively—our *tacit* or subconscious knowledge *(25, 47, 58)*. It is best to begin a theoretical approach to word knowledge by distinguishing between this type of knowledge and conscious, or *explicit* knowledge. In order to get a feel for this distinction, let's see how well we can answer this question: What rules do we follow when we use language? Perhaps the task can be made easier by considering subsidiary questions such as: How do we select the words that represent what we wish to say? How do we put these words together? How do we know that we should articulate the sound at the end of the word *tab* differently than the sound we articulate at the beginning of *bottle*? How do we know we can use the phrase "that mangy dog" and be assured that our listeners will know we are referring not to a dog at all but to our former business partner who last week absconded with the remaining company funds?

These questions about language are aimed at our tacit knowledge. We can speculate as to the answers; indeed, such speculation keeps linguists and many psychologists in business. Upon introspection, however, we cannot provide direct and unequivocal responses. In the case of language, as well as many aspects of our cognitive activity, there will always be substrata of knowledge beyond our conscious grasp; our "mind's eye" will be functionally blind. It is intriguing and a bit mysterious to reflect on knowledge we can never get at, but what is even more engaging about tacit knowledge is that it is *active*. Our brains are at work using this knowledge even when we are not consciously attempting to direct the thought process. This activity is analyzing, generalizing, and synthesizing to provide us with all manner of knowledge we could never have obtained through direct experience. Such activity allows us, as several theorists have noted, "to know more than we have learned" *(58)*.

To understand what words are it is necessary to understand and appreciate both tacit and explicit knowledge. Both children and adults know far more about words than they have actually learned. Most of the competence children bring to the task of dealing with the printed word is based on tacit knowledge, but there comes a point at which, for purposes of instruction, children must deal with words at an explicit level. How well teachers facilitate this transition depends in large measure on their appreciation of the nature of and interaction between these two types of knowledge. The linguistic and cognitive overview that we shall examine should aid in illuminating these processes of developing knowledge.

Word: A Linguistic Perspective

Any attempts to define "word" involve an obligatory qualification: It is just about impossible to do so in a clearcut, unequivocal fashion. Even if we restrict our definition to the English language (as we intend to do), we encounter difficulty. Consider, for example, the following definition from the *American Heritage Dictionary* (43):

> A sound, or combination of sounds, or its representation in writing or printing, that symbolizes and communicates a meaning and may consist of a single morpheme or of a combination of morphemes.*

We find this definition works fairly well until we run into *the*. Now, *the* is a unit which does not really "communicate a meaning," although most of us would probably agree that it is a word. If the word *the* has no meaning, what is it that language users must in some sense "know" about this or any word in order for it to assume its proper place in their mental lexicons? Miller has specified four categories of information that a word will typically possess: Pronunciation and spelling, syntactic role (part of speech), meaning, and restrictions upon usage. Keeping in mind the general focus of this monograph, in the sections that follow, we shall focus on pronunciation/spelling and meaning.

---

*Morphemes are considered to be the smallest meaningful units of language. The word *unacceptable*, for example, comprises three morphemes: *un, accept,* and *able*. Each morpheme conveys a particular meaning.

Linguistic theory has applied a fairly rigorous analysis to the quest of specifying what "words" are although, as we shall see, linguists have not always agreed on how much information they should take into account when trying to define and describe words. Before describing current linguistic contributions to the concept of *word*, it should be helpful to consider briefly the historical background from which the current theory has emerged. This will primarily serve the function of "free(ing) ourselves of certain commonly held misconceptions" (*38:3*) and, we might add, reaffirming some other sound intuitive conceptions we may have about the way words work.

Traditionally, American linguists have been concerned with "surface" aspects of language and words (*2, 34*). Their belief has been that linguistic phenomena are most reliably and validly investigated by paying scrupulous attention to what can be observed—speech. Those aspects having to do with the meaning that language conveys, and the role that meaning plays in determining the nature of observable speech, are not directly observable. Since these "unobservables" cannot be rigorously and empirically justified, they fall outside of the realm of linguistic enquiry.

Leonard Bloomfield (probably the most eminent American linguist of this theoretical persuasion), together with his theoretical offspring, directed their primary attention to the *phoneme*, or minimal speech sound. They analyzed the patterns and context in which phonemes can occur. Postal (*48*) has termed this type of analysis "autonomous phonemics" because the underlying assumption of the Bloomfieldians was that the ways in which phonemes occurred in speech could be understood primarily through phonemic analysis.

A few linguists, however, became dissatisfied with what they believed were limitations of the Bloomfieldian conception of language study. They held that there is simply too much going on in the stream of speech to be accounted for in terms of phonemic analysis. Thus, the linguistic school of *morphophonemics* developed (*53*). This theory held that, although meaning and syntax may not be directly observable in speech, they nevertheless have to play a role in determining how individuals use language and, more specifically, use words. The spirit of this movement can best be illustrated by (though it is by no means limited to) the following words: *record, content,*

Templeton

and *abstract*. One cannot know how to pronounce words such as these unless their meanings and syntactic functions are understood. We pronounce *record* with stress on the first syllable if we are talking about a plastic disc capable of reproducing music; we pronounce *record* with stress on the second syllable if we are talking about how the music came to be reproducible in the first place. Our pronunciation of *content* in the following sentence also depends on our knowledge of meaning and syntactic function. "The content of that sixpack has rendered Herbie content." Because we are assigning stress on the basis of meaning and syntactic function (form class), we are also changing the pronunciation of some of the phonemes in these words. The way in which phonemes are pronounced, therefore (phonemics), can be accounted for by the semantic and syntactic form (the "morph" in morphophonemics) of the word in which the phonemes occur.

Until recently, linguists did not usually concern themselves with how individuals acquire a language and structure that language within their brains. The linguistic theories of Chomsky (*11, 12, 13, 14*), however, have addressed such concerns and have helped to open up the domains of linguistic inquiry far beyond that of Bloomfield. Chomsky has pointed out that it is through language that we are able to discern the underlying creative aspect of human nature. This creativity may be what sets humans apart from other animals.

Chomsky has argued that human beings are capable of producing and understanding a potentially infinite number of sentences. With the exception of ritualized utterances such as "How's it going?" and "Good morning," most of the sentences we produce are original. Of course, the words have been used over and over, but the way in which the words are put together is different. Chomsky attributed this ability to create novel utterances to underlying syntactic (*deep*) structures that, together with transformational rules which change and combine these syntactic structures in various ways, allow the generation of an infinite number of sentences. These sentences constitute the *surface* structure of language.

The key to understanding Chomsky's theories and their implications for the human mind is expressed in a point of view Chomsky adopted from a group of Sixteenth Century French grammarians: We are able, by virtue of being human, to make infinite use of finite means (*18*). Moreover, Chomsky contends humans are innately predisposed to develop this finite system of language rules.

Where do words fit into Chomsky's theory? Because syntax is primary in the theory, words—and thus semantics—are considered merely to be *interpretive* elements. Words are catalogued in the lexicon which lists "... all the lexical items of the language and associates with each the (required) syntactic, semantic, and phonological information" (37:125). In the production of a sentence, words enter the picture only after syntactic deep structures have been transformed into a surface structure with a given number of lexical "slots." A set of syntactic features is associated with each slot. Items from the lexicon that have features similar to those associated with the lexical slots are then "inserted" into these slots. In Chomsky's theory, words as such are not the most important elements in language; they are merely surface structure phenomena.

For many years, Chomsky's theory was an awesome presence in linguistics. Because he was talking about underlying, deep structures and the creative aspect of human nature, he inevitably raised psychological questions as well. Psychologists set out to validate the psychological reality of transformations. Currently, however, this theory is under fire. Several inadequacies of the theory have been noted. Critics have suggested that the contributions of the "real world" have not been adequately incorporated into the theory, and that it does not deal realistically with the actual processes involved in producing and understanding language.

A more recent linguistic theory that has elevated words to a primary position is represented by *generative semantics* (*10, 21*). Generative semanticists have insisted that we are wasting time by considering syntactic transformations; these structures are not the bedrock of language ability. Rather, there are meaning or conceptual structures that underlie language—surface structures can give us an idea of the relationship among these underlying concepts, but the fundamental building blocks of language reflect concepts. As human beings, we label our underlying concepts with words. Generative semantics suggests, therefore, that language can be more promisingly studied by examining whatever cognitive structures words correspond to, together with the possible relationships that exist among words in the surface structure of language as well as among concepts at the deep structure, or meaning, level.

The task that linguists have now set for themselves is to specify what types of information humans would need to include in the lexical entry for each word. We noted earlier that our list comprising four categories of such information was minimal. Does this mean that we must include, for each and every word we know, a voluminous amount of information? Or might there be certain rules we can use for indicating how redundant or repetitive information about words that are similar in meaning can be extended to all such words? The following linguistic concepts help to define the problem.

Current linguistic theory has revived the notion of a *semantic* (55) consisting of lexical (word) and conceptual domains. Both domains cover a certain area of cognitive structure or, as Smith (51) has expressed it, "the theory of the world in our heads." Probably the most common example of a semantic field involves kinship relations. The lexical domain covering these relations includes words such as *mother, father, son, daughter, aunt, cousin*, and *nephew*. The conceptual domain includes both the underlying way the unique features or attributes of each lexical term are represented, as well as the ways in which these concepts are related in cognitive structure. In order to characterize a word such as *grandmother* as a lexical item we need semantic and relational features associated with its underlying concept. Semantic features for this word might include *animate, adult, female,* and *human.* Relational features would include those such as a *parent* whose children have children. There are semantic features associated with words which together with relational features help to locate each lexical item in an appropriate conceptual space.

Although we may not at this point have a clear picture of the lexicon, we may at least have a healthy appreciation of it and of the competence of the child to compile it. Before considering the cognitive theory that suggests the ways in which children come to know words at both the tacit and the explicit levels, we shall briefly describe some of the linguistic theories as they have been applied to English spelling.

Bloomfield (3), Hall (31), and Fries (26) believe spelling corresponds to the surface or spoken level of language, and that there is a fair degree of regularity between speech and print at this surface level. This regularity is illustrated by "word families" such as *hat/fat/mat* and *cake/lake/brake*. Words that do not follow such predictable patterns are deemed irregular. Bloomfield suggested that beginning instruction could take advantage of this regularity and fully acquaint the beginning reader with these highly predictable sound-to-spelling correspondences, postponing the irregular patterns until a later time.

Just as was the case with spoken language, linguists began to point out orthographic regularities that maintain correspondences among words at the syntactic and the semantic levels. Francis (*24*) cited word pairs such as *marine/mariner* and *advantage/advantageous*, stating that a "morphographic" relationship is maintained in such words, although the spoken forms might be phonetically quite different. What this means is that words that are similar in meaning are often similar in graphic structure. In a related vein, Venezky (*56*) described the "morphophonemic" aspects of English spelling, reflecting the gist of Francis's earlier observations. Venezky, however, explored the spelling system in more detail than Francis, and offered the first systematic analysis of English spelling to include a detailed investigation of the effects of syntax and meaning.

In *The Sound Pattern of English* (*15*) Chomsky and Halle offered quite an elegant theoretical explanation of English orthography. Their primary objective was to present a comprehensive overview of English phonology within a transformational-generative linguistic framework. English orthography, however, plays a fascinating role in their phonological theory. Because Chomsky and Halle's theory attempted to account for the variation in English spelling patterns in a more comprehensive fashion than have previous theories, we will examine it a bit more closely.

Chomsky and Halle claimed that, far from being irritatingly irregular, English orthography is nearly optimal for its purposes. They suggest that orthographic structure corresponds to a psychologically abstract level they term *lexical representation*, a level at which only enough phonological information is represented to predict the pronunciation of a word in various contexts. Each segment, or letter, in a word indirectly corresponds to an abstract segment in the lexical representation of that word. Like Francis's observation, Chomsky and Halle pointed out that words that are similar in meaning are *spelled* similarly; differences in pronunciation are a more superficial concern and can be handled by applying "intuitive phonological rules"—rules that, for the most part, individuals apply automatically.

To appreciate Chomsky and Halle's theory, it is necessary to probe further their concept of lexical representations. In a broad sense, lexical representations are supposed to reflect the way in which the basic units of our language are stored in our lexicon, or dictionary-in-the-head. Chomsky and Halle suggested that, in addition to minimal phonological information, lexical representations contain minimal syntactic specifications ("parts of speech" or roles each unit can fill) and semantic, or "meaning" features. Many words may derive from the same lexical item. *Elevation* and *elevator*, for example, derive from *elevate* which corresponds (with some adjustments) to the lexical representation in an individual's "dictionary." In theory, what this means is that a speaker of English does not need to store separately every vocabulary item in the lexicon; a large number of words do not have a separate entry but are derived from a single lexical item. In effect, this is quite an economical system.

Chomsky and Halle's theory differs from Francis's and Venezky's "morphographic" and "morphophonemic" theories in that it reflects operations at all cognitive and linguistic levels and brings them to bear on the relationship between the orthography and the mind. By considering more abstract relations that govern orthographic structure, Chomsky and Halle's theory accounts not only for structural similarities among words but for many of the apparent irrationalities of individual letter-sound spellings. In another paper in this monograph, Zutell discusses in more detail the implications of the theories of Venezky and of Chomsky and Halle for the learning of orthographic structure.

Word: A Cognitive Perspective

Language learning and the growth of vocabulary seem to occur almost automatically for most children. For many years, this development was described in terms such as "stimulus generalization," "chaining," and "extinction"—

terms used to explain a more superficial learning of language (*50, 52*). There is a rough parallel between this conception of language and the way in which linguists such as Bloomfield conceptualized language: One did not have to dig very deeply in the mind at all to explain the nature and acquisition of language. The notion of "mind" was ignored because, quite simply, it cannot be observed.

With the popularization of Piaget's developmental theory (*23, 46*), however, an hypothesized innate *linguistic* competence (the unobserved mind) appeared to be explained by underlying *cognitive* capabilities (*49*:11):

> ...it seems...more hopeful to suppose that the child brings to the task of acquiring his mother tongue a set of universal cognitive structures which have been built up during the first year of life and which provide enough assumptions about the nature of human language to enable the child to begin to join the talking community at about the age of one and one-half.

The apparent growth by leaps and bounds of spoken language, then, is merely the most obvious evidence of a correspondingly rapid growth in underlying cognitive structures. Piaget's work in what he terms *genetic epistemology*—the study of the development of knowledge structures—has allowed significant insight into how children come to know and use words.

In the previous section, we discussed the impossibility of defining a concept without relating it to other concepts. How is this system of relationships built up? How does the young child learn that, when the kitty's tail is pulled, a causal relationship exists between this event and the attributes of sound that follow (along with kitty's physical response—perhaps a rapid volley of slapping paws followed by flight to safer quarters)? Quite simply, the child learns these relationships through action. As Brown (*6*) and Halliday (*33*) have argued, these actions upon the world serve to structure the system of relations into which a first language will later fit. Most such relations are discovered during what Piaget terms the *sensorimotor* period (birth to approximately two and one-half years of age). During the following *preoperational* stage (approximately two and one-half to seven years of age), vocabulary will increase almost exponentially and syntactic structures will become more sophisticated.

The studies reported in this volume, and those articles that address instructional implications arising from the studies, involve children primarily at the preoperational and concrete operational levels. For this reason, these two stages will be briefly considered.

Preoperational children's thought is not bound by what is immediately present in the environment. The children are able to think about objects that are not present; thus, the early phases of this stage are characterized by what Piaget calls the "construction of the permanent object." The semiotic, or symbolic, function develops progressively during this stage, accounting in part for the tremendous growth of language. What Piaget would term the qualitative development of cognitive structure, or schemata, depends not so much on the child's mental manipulations of symbolic representations but, rather, on the continued interaction with objects and events in the child's immediate environment. Indeed, according to Piaget, it is not until around the ages of eleven or twelve, that language per se becomes an active and valuable agent in the higher-order thought processes of an individual.

Preoperational children are governed by perception. They are attuned to the apparent features of whatever stimuli they are observing. Concrete operational children, on the other hand, are more conceptually oriented. They can transform objects and events in a variety of ways without actually having to perceive these transformations in the immediate present. Preoperational children are sensitive to states of things in the immediate present. They do not understand transformations from one state to another; if a ball of clay is rolled into the shape of a snake, there is more clay than there was before because it looks like there is more clay—the effect of the transformation is superseded by what is now observable. The concrete operational child, on the other hand, is able to suspend judgment based on perception of states, so that the effects of transformations are included. In Flavell's terms (22), *perceived appearances* are superceded by *inferred reality*. In effect, although concrete operational children's perceptions are relating one type of information, they are able to transcend the immediate stimulus and infer the actual condition. This ability allows the concrete operational child to effect an extremely important cognitive trick: The child is able to *decenter* attention from one salient feature of a stimulus to consider simultaneously several featural attributes. The preoperational child is unable to do this. With perceptual mechanisms locked into one type of information, the child cannot be freed from that one aspect of the stimulus.

The ability to decenter represents a major growth in cognitive capacity. To illustrate, whereas preoperational children may tell you that a word is something that "comes out of your mouth" (*54*), concrete operational children are more likely to tell you that a word may be spoken or written, is made up of sounds or letters, and stands for something. They can simultaneously attend to a variety of features. Importantly— from the standpoint of learning about words and the reading process in general—concrete operational children are able to think about language as an object of study in itself, and are able to approach it analytically. Preoperational children, by the very nature of their cognitive schemata, are unable to do so. Being egocentric, they tend to define the world in terms of perceived features as these features relate to their own subjective world. Being unable to be "objective" in any adult sense of the term, they cannot pull back from the immediate present and reflect on matters. This is the case with language— even more so, perhaps. Language is not objectified in the environment for children. It is something that is automatic and a part of children's subjective selves. It is always inextricably bound up within every activity and is a part of that activity. It is never "out there" in the sense that children can look at it and gradually begin to differentiate themselves from it.

Piaget has suggested that both preoperational and concrete operational children are capable of thinking at levels that are qualitatively richer than their corresponding ability to verbalize might indicate. Although this claim has not gone uncontested (*42*), it does seem to apply at least to the level of tacit knowledge discussed earlier. For example, despite children's inability to consciously analyze language, they certainly are capable of interacting with print in suprisingly productive ways, as several of the studies in this monograph suggest. Piaget would probably claim that emphasizing printed language prior to the attainment of formal operational thought does not lead to the development of higher-order thought processes (27). It can be argued that the study of the structure of printed language, specifically words (44), may certainly contribute to such higher-order development. Indeed, those attempts to relate Piagetian theory to children's encounters with the printed word have perhaps overemphasized the *explicit* side of the knowledge coin and have ignored the *tacit* (5, 20, 27). To analyze words productively at a conscious level, children should be able to understand that the letter is a complex concept that is usually part of a larger entity, such as a word. The correspondence between the letter and sound is not one-to-one; the letter *a*, for example, will represent different sounds in different graphemic contexts. Failure to grasp this concept, as we have indicated, does not mean we should shield children from print until we think they have arrived at concrete operations. To do so is to ignore their tacit knowledge of letters, words, and printed language as a whole.

Word: A Tentative Synthesis

We have explored both the structure of words and the elusive conceptual domain to which they correspond. We have also considered the theory underlying the cognitive competencies that children are able to apply to the consideration of words. What implications for children's word knowledge arise from the intersection of linguistic and cognitive theory?

With respect to the child's initial learning of words or language, we can define two points between which our theories will operate. On the one hand is Brown's "original word game" (7). In this game, words function as "pointers" for the beginning language learners, indicating what features of the environment the adult community believes are important—worthy enough to be named, if you will. Adults have the word *stove*, for example; this indicates to the young child that there is some important thing out there that will serve the child well to learn about. For the child, these spoken utterances are labels for the world; the child's task is to seek out those aspects of the world that have been deemed worthy enough to be labeled.

On the other hand, we have the position articulated by McNamara (39) which holds that children must first structure a fairly rich system of meaning categories before any type of language can begin to play a part in signalling features of the environment. These categories must somehow be constructed without linguistic prompts or cues of any kind. Although McNamara's hypothesis appears to be quite close to the Piagetian perspective discussed earlier, the two are not in complete accord. It is true that some type of semantic categorization must precede language learning, but even the young infant is attuned to the "highlighting" features of adult language in announcing the presence of objects or events. Rules are borrowed from both Brown's and McNamara's extremes and effectively synthesized. Much work will go into learning the label for a particular class of objects and refining the rules by which new objects are identified with that label. Let us consider what is involved.

In learning a word, children have two sources of data available to them. First, they have the linguistic context in which the word occurs—the total utterance. Second, they have the situation or environmental context in which the word is used. The children must follow certain "procedures" (*41*) to see if a certain object is to be labeled with a certain word. The conceptual domain to which the word representing that object comes to correspond usually consists of two parts, according to Miller and Johnson—Laird (*41*:696):

> a *definitional* part depending on a functional-perceptual schema for recognizing instances (the "procedures" we have discussed) and a *connotative* part consisting of knowledge associated with the word, *including the relation of the concept to other concepts* [emphasis added].

These "functional-perceptual" schemata arise out of experience with the world—action, as Piaget would emphasize. The more children interact with their world, the more procedures they will have for applying a wider and more finely-differentiated battery of perceptual tests.

We are conceptualizing a dynamic, continually changing state of affairs insofar as "word knowledge" is concerned. By applying an analysis—resting in cognitive theory—of the way in which children come to know about their world to a consideration of how lexical entries are represented—the concern of linguists, we recall—we have arrived at a promising synthesis. The linguist's problem is to identify the features or attributes with which lexical entries may be specified. We can now appreciate that these features or attributes are not static entities that are inherent in the world; rather, they consist in large measure of the *perceptual tests* we have mentioned—lists of the dynamic interactions we have had with lamps, food processors, polyester shirts, and gophers. In addition, we have rules for relating these entries to one another, procedures which themselves are abstracted from our perceptual tests of the world.

What about those things we have not directly experienced, or cannot experience (in a "hands-on" sense) by their very nature—such as time? As Clark (*16*) has suggested, we appear to extend a related perceptual experience to include the new lexical item. In the case of time, the closest analogy our conceptual domain can generate is distance or length, concepts that are understood through actual perceptual tests. It is no accident that we have applied the concept of a line, a perceptually experienced entity, to represent the concept of time.

Our bottom line, of course, is the two dimensional representation of lexical items ordered by orthographic structure. How do the linguistic and cognitive theories we have discussed apply to children's encounters with print? The process begins long before children encounter kindergarten and readiness programs.

If you have watched babies interact with a two dimensional representation you will notice they evidence application of three dimensional perceptual tests: they try to pick up an object in a picture, polka dots on a blouse, or a spot of light on the floor. One of their more delightful tests is described by Henderson in Chapter One—taking note of the front view of a cow or a lamb on a page in a book, they will turn the page over in search of the hindquarters. They come to learn, however, that much of the world is represented in two dimensional arrays, and print is a two dimensional ubiquitous presence in their world. Indeed, they can create two dimensional representations early (*30*). The consequence of this "fundamental graphic act" are the perceptual tests that define the distinctive features of print. This suggests that, from a very early age, "exploring with a pencil"—as Clay (*17*) has aptly referred to the enterprise—is a critically important activity, one that will eventually allow words to be concretely and intellectually experienced.

Piagetian theory suggests that, particularly for young children, a considerable amount of hands-on involvement is required of any experience before that experience can be consciously examined and discussed. It is difficult to get one's hands on language. Language is transparent (9); whatever transformations it undergoes are not nearly as perceptually real as, for example, rolling out a ball of clay. Print appears to play a crucial but paradoxical role in turning the transparency of spoken language into the opaqueness of an object that can be studied—paradoxical because print is supposed to be a second order abstraction from reality, with spoken language being a first order abstraction. Logically, it would appear that print would be more difficult to grasp conceptually than spoken language. If we assume that to understand print entails a fairly elaborate explanation of its characteristics and function, then print may indeed be more difficult. If on the other hand we admit the virtues of tacit knowledge, then we see where print, by being a common and fairly stable symbolic system in the environment, draws the young child's attention toward the abstract symbolic structure of language. Print freezes the continuous stream of speech into perceptually manipulable blocks and begins to pull a child's tacit knowledge about words to the surface where an explicit understanding can begin to develop. As Papandropoulou and Sinclair (45:257) state, "...the written word is in a sense a permanent result and, moreover, an objective product of verbal activity." Ehri (19:211) extended this notion: "...lexical awareness...is simply awakened as a consequence of reading print" as opposed to being "acquired *and shaped* by experience with printing conventions" [emphasis added].

As we have seen, language frozen in print leads not only to a tacit recognition of language characteristics but to the production of this second order system. Long before children can explicitly deal with what Elkind (20) has termed the "complex logical construction" of the letter, they use letters to represent speech. This is a competence predicted by theories of tacit knowledge and it naturally follows from the earliest perceptual tests of the fundamental graphic act. This competence, together with other tacit notions about print and words, will allow children eventually to become "metalinguistically aware." When children come to see both their own written productions and the words that others may write from more than one perspective, they should be able to understand the transformations allowed by standard English orthography; moreover, their explicit word knowledge should increase exponentially. In other words, children can mentally race from thinking of words in terms of sound-print relationships to thinking of them in terms of reference, and back again. They can appreciate the initial consonant substitution games that teachers play with them because they are able to understand the transformations involved in going from *bat* to *cat* to *fat* and back again to *bat.*

Piaget, as well as Vygotsky (*57*)—who is often held to be diametrically opposed to Piaget—holds that a qualitatively more powerful intellect develops from about the ages of eleven or twelve. Cognitive theory, therefore, would predict the following: Just as language in and of itself may from this point onward be used as a potent means of stimulating thought so, too, may the orthographic structure of the language come to have symbolic primacy in a person's mental dictionary. What this means is that for many of us, most readily accessible information about words may be accessed through our knowledge of spelling, as opposed to sound or structure. It does not require the credentials of contemporary cognitive and linguistic theory to offer support for this notion. In 1919, Bradley (*4*:16), Editor of the *Oxford Dictionary*, offered the following comment in referring to many words that occur more often in print than in speech:

> ... the normal relation between alphabetic writing and speech is simply reversed; *the group of letters is the real word*, and the pronunciation merely its symbol [emphasis added].

There is a parallel between this sensitivity to higher order orthographic structure and the young child learning words. The linguist's idea of a conceptual core that underlies and relates (for example, the words *shoe, moccasin,* and *boot*) applies equally well to the learning of more abstract or "economical" orthographic patterns in words (*29*). For example, words such as *misogynist* and *gynecocracy* share a common conceptual core, one that is easily discernible if we know where or how to look. If older individuals have not established an efficient set of procedures that can be applied to word structure, they are deprived of exploring the structure and content of orthographic regularity. They do not perceive the various ways in which meaning is visually preserved in related words despite gross variations in pronunciation. In other words, they have no way of getting to the conceptual core. With respect to higher order orthographic structure, we can be fairly definite about the implications, both theoretical and practical. The procedures for examining orthographic structure offer considerable promise for economizing our mental dictionaries (and, by extension, more efficiently organizing our "theories of the world").

Recall our earlier statement about tacit and explicit knowledge: We know far more than we have learned. In the case of young children, we have developed this argument: Children will use the print that surrounds them (as well as some judiciously offered advice from a parent or teacher) to generate a powerful knowledge of print. With regard to word structure, how does the dictum hold true for older individuals? By applying procedures for examining orthographic structure, these individuals' tacit knowledge will be stimulated to rearrange concepts (the linguist's *conceptual domains*) in any number of novel orientations. This idea is further elaborated in the discussions by Zutell and Templeton (Chapters Five and Seven).

What the more prominent aspects of cognitive and linguistic theory suggest, and what a substantial body of research seems to be affirming, is that children are able to approach written language and its most distinguished element, the word, with an impressive array of abilities. The types of word knowledge we often see children evidence in the classroom may very well not be the type of knowledge we would expect on a tacit level. What we see is a reflection of our notions of which orthographic units are worthy of children's study, arranged in a sequence we feel is desirable. It is worthy, therefore, to ask questions about competence, as most of the theories we have considered have done. Herein lies perhaps the greatest value of these theories: Questions of competence yield more comprehensible answers to otherwise puzzling performance, some examples of which are discussed in the investigations of young children's invented spelling.

By way of summary, we see that understanding a particular word posits a complex underlying structure that includes *form*, characteristic of the lexical domain, and *substance*, characteristic of the conceptual domain. When we understand the substance of word, in terms of definition (identification) procedures and connotative aspects, we do so on the basis of active encounters with objects, events, properties, and relations. When we understand the form of a word we do so on the basis of active encounters with the "internal grammar" (*29*) of that form. Our procedures are therefore applied both to the substance and the form of words.

Although instruction often assumes our knowledge of words is based on copying reality, we see that this cannot be the case. We may be tricked, however, into believing this is so and in such fashion be cut off from attempts to develop more sophisticated tests and procedures; our explicit knowledge is not allowed to take advantage of a rich vein of tacit knowledge. But we are coming more and more to talk of pedagogical matters, and the articles that follow will deal with those concerns.

What is a word? Theory gives us a fair idea concerning how we might ask the question and generate some hypotheses. It is time to turn to the children for some possible answers.

References

1. Bierwisch, M. "Semantics," in J. Lyons (Ed.), *New Horizons in Linguistics*. Harmmondsworth, Middlesex, England: Penguin Books, 1970.
2. Bloomfield, L. *Language*. New York: Holt, Rinehart and Winston, 1933.
3. Bloomfield, L. "Linguistics and Reading," *Elementary English*, 19 (1942), 125-130, 183-186.
4. Bradley, H. *On the Relations between Spoken and Written Language*. Oxford: Clarendon Press, 1919.
5. Briggs, C., and D. Elkind. "Cognitive Development in Early Readers," *Developmental Psychology*, 9 (1973), 279-280.
6. Brown, R. *A First Language: The Early Stages*. Cambridge, Massachusetts: Harvard University Press, 1973.
7. Brown, R. "The Original Word Game," Appendix in J. Bruner, J. Goodnow, and G. Austin, *A Study of Thinking*. New York: John Wiley, 1956.
8. Cahen, L., M. Craun, and S. Johnson. "Spelling Difficulty: A Survey of the Research," *Review of Educational Research*, 41, 281-301.
9. Cazden, C. "Play and Metalinguistic Awareness," *Urban Review*, 1973.
10. Chafe, W. *Meaning and the Structure of Language*. Chicago: University of Chicago Press, 1970.
11. Chomsky, N. *Aspects of the Theory of Syntax*. Cambridge, Massachusetts: The MIT Press, 1965.

12. Chomsky, N. *Language and Mind*. New York: Harcourt Brace Jovanovich, 1968.
13. Chomsky, N. *Syntactic Structures*. The Hague: Mouton, 1957.
14. Chomsky, N. *Reflections on Language*. New York: Random House, 1975.
15. Chomsky, N., and M. Halle. *The Sound Pattern of English*. New York: Harper and Row, 1968.
16. Clark, H.H. "Space, Time, Semantics, and the Child," in T. Moore (Ed.), *Cognitive Development and the Acquisition of Language*. New York: Academic Press, 1973.
17. Clay, M. "Exploring with a Pencil," *Theory into Practice*, 1976.
18. denOuden, B.D. *Language and Creativity: An Interdisciplinary Essay in Chomskian Humanism*. Lisse, Netherlands: Peter deRidder Press, 1975.
19. Ehri, L.C. "Word Consciousness in Readers and Prereaders," *Journal of Educational Psychology*, 67 (1975), 204-212.
20. Elkind, D. "Cognitive Development and Reading," paper presented at the annual convention of the International Reading Association, New Orleans, 1974.
21. Fillmore, C.J. "The Case for Case," in E. Bach and R.T. Harms (Eds.), *Universals of Linguistic Theory*. New York: Holt, Rinehart and Winston, 1968.
22. Flavell, J. *Cognitive Development*. Englewood Cliffs, New Jersey: Prentice-Hall, 1977.
23. Flavell, J. *The Developmental Psychology of Jean Piaget*. Princeton, New Jersey: Van Nostrand, 1963.
24. Francis, W.N. *The Structure of American English*. New York: Ronald Press, 1958.
25. Franks, J.J. "Toward Understanding Understanding," in W. Weimer and D. Palermo (Eds.), *Cognition and the Symbolic Processes*. Hillsdale, New Jersey: Lawrence Erlbaum, 1974.
26. Fries, C. *Linguistics and Reading*. New York: Holt, Rinehart and Winston, 1963.
27. Furth, H. "Reading as Thinking: A Developmental Perspective," in F. Murray and J. Pikulski (Eds.), *The Acquisition of Reading*. Baltimore: University Park Press, 1978.
28. Gibson, E. "Trends in Perceptual Development: Implications for the Reading Process," in A. Pick (Ed.), *Minnesota Symposia on Child Psychology*, 8 (1974), 24-54.
29. Gibson, E., and H. Levin. (Eds.) *The Psychology of Reading*. Cambridge, Massachusetts: MIT Press, 1975.
30. Gibson, J., and P. Yonas. "A New Theory of Scribbling and Drawing in Children," *The Analysis of Reading Skills*. Final Report, Project No. 5-1212, Cornell University and U.S. Office of Education, December 1968, 355-370.
31. Hall, R.A. *Sound and Spelling in English*. New York: Chilton, 1961.
32. Halle, M. "Preface," in M. Halle, J. Bresnan, and G.a. Miller (Eds.) *Linguistic Theory and Psychological Reality*. Cambridge, Massachusetts: MIT Press, 1978.
33. Halliday, M.A.K. *Learning How to Mean: Explorations in the Development of Language*. New York: Elsevier, 1975.
34. Hockett, C.G. *The State of the Art*. The Hague: Mouton, 1968.
35. Jackendoff, R. "Toward an Explanatory Semantic Representation," *Linguistic Inquiry*, 7 (1976), 89-150.

36. Kintsch, W. *The Representation of Meaning in Memory.* Hillsdale, New Jersey: Lawrence Erlbaum, 1974.
37. Lyons, J. "Generative Syntax," in J. Lyons (Ed.), *New Horizons in Linguistics.* Harmmondsworth, Middlesex, England: Penguin Books, 1970.
38. Lyons, J. *Introduction to Theoretical Linguistics.* Cambridge, Massachusetts: University Press, 1968.
39. McNamara, J. "Cognitive Basis of Language Learning in Infants," *Psychological Review,* 79 (1972), 1-13.
40. Miller, G.A. "Semantic Relations among Words," in M. Halle, J. Bresnan, and G.A. Miller (Eds.), *Linguistic Theory and Psychological Reality.* Cambridge, Massachusetts: MIT Press, 1978.
41. Miller, G.A., and P. Johnson-Laird. *Language and Perception.* Cambridge, Massachusetts: Harvard University Press, 1976.
42. Miller, S.A. "Nonverbal Assessment of Piagetian Concepts," *Psychological Bulletin,* 83 (1976), 405-430.
43. Morris, W. (Ed). *The American Heritage Dictionary.* Boston: Houghton-Mifflin, 1976.
44. Murray, F.B. "Implications of Piaget's Theory for Reading Instruction," in S.J. Samuels (Ed.), *What Research Has to Say about Reading Instruction.* Newark, Delaware: International Reading Association, 1978.
45. Papandropoulou, I., and H. Sinclair. "What Is a Word? Experimental Study of Children's Ideas on Grammar," *Human Development,* 17 (1974), 241-258.
46. Piaget, J., and B. Inhelder. *The Psychology of the Child.* New York: Basic Books, 1969.
47. Polanyi, M. *The Tacit Dimension.* New York: Doubleday, 1966.
48. Postal, P. *Aspects of Phonological Theory.* New York: Harper and Row, 1968.
49. Sinclair deZwart, H. "Language Acquisition and Cognitive Development," in T. Moore (Ed.), *Cognitive Development and the Acquisition of Language.* New York: Academic Press, 1973.
50. Skinner, B.F. *Verbal Behavior.* New York: Appleton-Century-Crofts, 1957.
51. Smith, F. *Understanding Reading,* Second Edition. New York: Holt, Rinehart and Winston, 1978.
52. Staats, A.W., and C.K. Staats. *Complex Human Behavior: A Systematic Extension of Learning Principles.* New York: Holt, Rinehart and Winston, 1963.
53. Swadesh, M., and C.F. Voegelin. "A Problem in Phonological Alternation," *Language,* 15 (1939), 1-10.
54. Templeton, S., and E.M. Spivey. "The Concept of Word in Young Children as a Function of Level of Cognitive Developments," *Research in the Teaching of English* (in press).
55. Trier, J. *Der deutsche Wortschatz im Sinnbezirk des Verstandes.* Heidelberg, 1931.
56. Venezky, R. *The Structure of English Othography.* The Hague: Mouton, 1970.
57. Vygotsky, L.S. *Thought and Language.* Edited and translated by E. Haufmann and G. Vakar. Cambridge, Massachusetts: MIT Press, 1962.
58. Weimer, W. "Psycholinguistics and Plato's Paradoxes of the Meno," *American Psychologist,* 28 (1974), 15-33.

Chapter Three

Developmental Strategies of Spelling Competence in Primary School Children

James W. Beers
College of William and Mary

In the past, learning to spell was viewed as a serial learning task coupled necessarily with the proper pronunciation of spelling words. The work of Furness (6), for instance, appeared to show that mispronunciation of words leads to misspellings. Similarly, Jensen (7) concluded that serial learning effects could predict the occurrence of spelling errors in words of varying lengths. Recently, an alternative hypothesis about how children learn to spell has moved away from this mechanistic view. The thrust of this hypothesis is that learning to spell like learning to speak and read is a language based activity. Following a model akin to the generative-transformational grammar model, researchers now hypothesize that children internalize information about spoken and written words, organize that information, construct tentative rules based on that information, and apply these rules to the spelling of words.

This hypothesis has been tested in several recent studies in which the spelling strategies of preschoolers and primary grade children have been studied. Read (8) examined the spelling attempts of preschool children in the Boston area and found in their attempts a heavy reliance on the preschoolers' phonological knowledge of spoken English. Read also concluded that orthographic knowledge is acquired systematically and not haphazardly. There was little evidence of random spelling errors. The errors that occurred were consistent with virtually every spelling condition and child that Read examined. Read believes that children know how sounds are articulated and use that knowledge in their early spelling attempts. He concluded that early spelling strategies were replaced by later ones which reflected the application of phonological knowledge and not simple letter-phoneme association. For example, long vowels initially appeared for short vowel sounds (MAT-met), followed later by short vowel for long vowel sounds (MIT-meet) as the children attempted to represent vowel elements in written English. Read reasoned that positions of articulation for letter names and sounds represented by letters were readily used by the children in his sample as they sought the correct spelling of words.

Read (9) later examined six and seven year old children's ability to recognize phonetic similarities among sounds and to represent these sounds orthographically. The children in the study were presented with a nonsense word and a pair of real words. They were instructed to select from each pair the word that "sounded like" the nonsense word. First graders commonly matched a short vowel word with a word containing a similar sounding long vowel. For example [pek] was matched more often with *peck* rather than *peek*. The seven year olds also made matches between certain short vowels. For example, the nonsense word [stIp] was matched with *step* more often than *steep*. Read concluded that this shift away from short-long vowel matching was due to maturational factors or the effects of first and second grade instruction in reading and spelling.

Another finding in this study revealed that adults do not necessarily make the same phonetic judgments about sounds and spelling as primary school children do. If this is an accurate assessment of children's recognition of phonetic relationships, then teachers may assign inappropriate reasons for a primary age child's word recognition or spelling attempts. Most reading and spelling programs utilize phonetic analysis, and yet many children may not categorize English sounds according to this conventional analysis.

Beers and Henderson (2) analyzed the spelling attempts of first grade children in one classroom in Laurel, Maryland, over a six month period. Very specific orthographic conditions were examined which included short and long vowel spellings (*get, gate*), morphological markers (*ing, ed, er*) and various consonant spellings. By noting the spelling changes in weekly creative writing stories for each condition over a six month period, several sequential strategies emerged for most of the children examined. Examples of the spelling sequences can be seen in Table 1.

Table 1
Spelling Pattern Sequence in Selected Categories

Short *e* as in *met*
1. *a* for *e* - GAT (*get*)
2. *i* for *e* - WINT (*went*)
3. correct form

Short *i* as in *sit*
1. *e* for *i* - MES (*miss*)
2. correct form - MIS (*miss*)

Long *a* as in *gate*
1. correct form - GAT (*gate*)
2. *e* for *a* - GET (*gate*)
3. *ay* or *ae* for *a* - GAETT (*gate*)
4. correct form - GATE

Long *e* as in *feet*
1. *e* for *ee* - FET (*feet*)
2. *i* for *ee* - FIT (*feet*)
3. *ea* for *ee* - FEAT (*feet*)
4. correct form

Nasal consonants - single letter
1. correct form when not part of a blend - CAM (*came*), MENE (*many*)
2. omitted when part of a blend - JOP (*jump*), WAT (*went*)
3. emergence of *m, n* in consonant blend - WANT (*went*)

Flaps as in *patter* and *later*
1. *d* for *t* or *tt* - PIDER (*pitter*), SWEDER (*sweater*)
2. *t* for *tt* or *tt* for *t* - BITTIG (*biting*), LITL (*little*)

Morphological ending
ed as in *wasted*
1. *d* substituted for *ed* - PETD (*painted*)
2. *id, ud, ad* for *ed* - STARETID (*started*)

ed as in *passed*
1. *t* for *ed* - NOCT (*knocked*)
2. *et* for *ed* - DRESET (*dressed*)

Beers

Initially, position or articulation played a major role in many of the spelling patterns examined which demonstrated that these children also relied on their knowledge of how English sounds are articulated. The letter-name strategy saw the most appropriate letter-name being substituted for a particular sound. These letter-name spellings can be seen in FET for *fit* and PAN for *pen*.

Another example of the children's awareness of English can be seen in their spelling of nasal consonants. In an initial position, medial position or final position *m* or *n* appeared correctly (MENE for many). When either was part of a consonant blend, however, the *m* or *n* was omitted (JUP for jump). Articulation features appear to be the main reason for this consistent omission since nasals are articulated in the position that is used for a consonant that immediately follows the nasal. This explains why a syllable *m* appears before *p* and *b* consonants, *n* before *d* and *t* and *n* as in *ing* before *g* and *k*. Perhaps it is an internalized awareness that the articulation positions for these final consonants are the major influence upon the nasals that causes less concern for the nasal itself in the children's own knowledge of the English sound system.

A second strategy saw the emergence of an awareness of letters representing sounds rather than being sounds themselves. Short vowels began to appear spelled correctly and pre-consonant nasals now regularly appeared. There was still an awareness of the phonological nature of written language although graphemic constraints were being considered by the children at this level.

Finally, a transitional stage appeared in the spellings where the use of orthographic markers (MAED for *made* or PAETT for *pat*) and morphophonemic elements was common in most spellings. The children at this stage were combining information based on knowledge about English sounds, morphemes in written words, and syntax in order to spell words in their creative writing. For example, in the sentence "My dad is raking the leavz" the *z* in *leavz* represents the plural form phonetically, not as a distinct morpheme. The writer also retained the silent *e* in *raking* but omitted it in *leaves*. Children at this transitional stage have not yet learned how English spelling is affected by meaning and syntax, but they are moving away from the idea that pronunciation is the major control on English spelling.

These data also revealed that the children appeared to proceed through many of these spelling pattern sequences at different rates. Some children would pass through the initial step of a particular sequence more rapidly than others, while other children would appear to skip an initial step as though they were more advanced in spelling a particular orthographic configuration. It was found, however, that the sequence of steps for the spelling patterns examined appeared constant for most of the children. For example, the pupils who began to write in February used the level one strategy for a spelling pattern that the November writer used. This observation indicates that later beginning writers follow the same spelling pattern sequences seen in earlier beginning writers. It would appear, therefore, that the spelling pattern sequences are generally invariant regardless of when a child begins to write.

These spelling pattern sequences suggest that children seem to have developed a highly sophisticated knowledge of English phonology. They are acutely aware of the characteristics of English sounds and have established a hierarchy of these characteristics with which to base their initial spelling of English words. The fact that the sequences are relatively consistent indicates that they may be building a set of internalized rules with which to deal with the system of English orthography. It would appear that the child's growing knowledge of English words is not based on simple letter-sound correspondences but on a combination of phonological and syntactic information as it applies to spoken and written language.

A subsequent study (1) attempted to statistically validate the spelling noted in the Read and Beers and Henderson studies. One of the difficulties encountered in these two earlier studies was the inability to control what words were spelled by the children or the frequency with which the words were spelled. By controlling these variables, it was hoped that this later study could answer several important questions. First, when asked to spell selected words over a six month period of time, do first and second graders advance as predicted from no attempt, to letter-name spellings, to transitional errors and, finally, correct spellings? Second, what differences occur as a function of high and low frequency in words of comparable length and phonetic structure?

A spelling word list was given to 75 first graders and 70 second graders in Charlottesville, Virginia, once a month between January and May 1974. These children were representative middle class primary school pupils following a standard basal reader curriculum of instruction. Four single syllable words were selected for each of six spelling categories which were long *a (take), e (seat* or *week), i (wide* or *light);* short *a (hat), e (met),* and *i (sit).* Two of the words in each category were from the 500 most frequently used words according to the Lorge-Thorndike Word List *(10)* and two were below the 1,000 most frequently used words.

The spelling attempts by the children received a score of 1 to 4. These scores represented the sequential pattern of errors seen in the vowels' spellings in the Read and Beers and Henderson studies. This sequence can be seen in an explanation of the scores. A *1* was given for the omission of the vowel element, *2* for a letter-name spelling, *3* for a transitional-type spelling, and *4* for the correct rendering of the vowel element and its marker if necessary.

The results of a sign test performed on the monthly scores in each child's spellings indicated that a significantly greater number of children's scores changed sequentially on 23 of the 24 words (see Table 2). There were very few children who showed no change from a low score. The majority of those children who made no changes for specific words spelled them correctly throughout the study.

The analysis of variance in each vowel category indicated that the spelling scores of first graders differed significantly from second graders' scores across all vowel categories. A test of the simple effects of time on the two grades revealed that the first graders moved consistently from lower to high scores while many second graders scored consistently on four vowel categories. The high frequency words received higher scores than low frequency words in all but the short *i* category. The difference between high and low frequency word scores was greatest in the first graders' spelling attempts throughout the study.

Table 2
Sign Tests on Sequential Scores of the 24 Spelling Words

Word	Sequence	No Sequence	No Change	Z
gate	60	28	57	3.4*
lake	80	24	41	5.4*
drape	87	34	24	4.4*
spade	84	34	27	4.2*
week	54	27	64	2.7*
seat	94	34	17	5.8*
streak	106	38	1	6.0*
creek	94	31	20	6.3*
light	87	32	26	5.8*
ride	57	13	75	5.0*
tribe	86	35	24	4.2*
dike	80	28	37	4.8*
back	53	16	76	5.2*
hat	30	11	104	5.0*
sap	66	28	51	3.8*
stack	61	23	61	4.4*
bed	45	13	87	3.4*
step	86	18	41	6.6*
speck	91	23	31	6.0*
wreck	81	40	24	3.4*
lip	75	26	44	4.8*
stick	61	36	48	2.4*
pit	75	21	48	5.4*
lid	57	52	36	0.4

*$p < .01$

Several conclusions were drawn from the results of this study. Children between the ages of six and seven years do follow sequential spelling strategies that progress as the youngster develops. The sequence of strategies was most common in first graders for several reasons. A large number of second graders spelled many words correctly throughout the study, which would preclude any sequence in their spelling. In this study it should also be remembered that the scoring system employed was based on the results of the study by Beers and Henderson which had only examined the spelling attempts of a class of first grade children.

The fact that such spelling pattern sequences were found in this larger sample of children might suggest something about the developmental nature of learning to spell. According to Piaget, many six year old children are still in the stage of preoperational thought which precedes the stage of concrete operations in his theory of cognitive development. One of the primary characteristics of a child at the preoperational level is his centering on the single most dominant characteristic of an object. This centration causes many real objects to be perceived as one dimensional. The inability to perceive other salient features of objects seems to have been reflected in the extremely common use of the letter-name strategy by many first grade children in the early stages of this study. These children were aware of letters but only by their respective letter names. The name of the letter became the single most dominantly used feature to spell vowel elements in all the vowel categories for these children.

The ability of many second graders to use information about high frequency words when faced with spelling low frequency words may account for the fact that second graders consistently spelled all words better than first graders. Second graders generally have a greater sight vocabulary, basic word knowledge and experience with writing words and could apply this knowledge to unfamiliar words.

The transference of information about known words to unknown words may lend some validity to Chomsky's notion of lexical representations and learning to spell. The Piagetian concept of cognitive development may even provide a structure for what Chomsky believed six and seven year olds do with words. Chomsky (4) hypothesized that six year olds do not know everything about the rules that govern the pronunciation of English words. Through repeated exposure to written words the child will gradually internalize enough information about similarly spelled words that may have different pronunciations. The child will link this information about similar words to the lexical representations that correspond closely to written words so he can begin to spell correctly words that have similar lexical representations but different pronunciations.

By the time a child has been continually exposed to written words and their similar letter combinations with different pronunciations, he needs to have a cognitive framework that can make use of these kinds of information. The seven year old who deals in concrete operations has the beginnings for such a framework. He can deal with the surface characteristics of written words and categorize types of words by their orthographic features. He need not be restricted to pronunciation, as he is at an earlier age.

For a child to have lexical spellings continually emerge as correctly spelled words would require an extensive examination of words over a considerable length of time. It would appear, therefore, that a higher level of abstract thinking may be needed to spell unfamiliar words correctly and consistently. It may be that a child through continued exposure to words and types of words finally achieves a more or less complete understanding of written language at the age that formal operations occur in Piaget's theory of development. It may be that such understanding is not totally grasped until this period of development.

The results of a final study (3) indicate that these spelling strategies occur not only in first and second graders' writings but in third and fourth graders' spelling attempts. A list of five high and five low frequency words representing five vowel categories (short *a, e, i;* long *a* and *i*) was given to children in grades one through four enrolled in various schools in Michigan. They had been exposed to different kinds of reading and spelling instruction. The youngsters' misspellings revealed overwhelming reliance on the letter-name strategy in the early grades. The percentage of youngsters using this strategy steadily dropped from second to fourth grade, although some fourth graders still relied on the strategy. The other two strategies which were also found in the earlier studies saw the attempt to use vowel markers like silent *e* and the substitution of one short vowel for another similar short vowel.

This study once again points to the developmental nature of learning to spell. Probably the most significant evidence for this conclusion lies in the way in which the children differed in their spelling of high and low frequency words. Many of the high frequency words were spelled correctly (*hat, bed, gate*) which can be attributed to reading or spelling instruction. These very same children, however, failed to spell the low frequency words correctly (*sap, speck, drape*) regardless of the classroom instruction they had received. This finding suggests that, although children may memorize weekly spelling lists, they may not yet recognize the orthographic principles underlying those words; otherwise, they would certainly apply them to less familiar words. This ability to develop and apply the principles of English orthography brings us back to the original hypothesis stated at the beginning of this paper.

Over an extended period of time children internalize what they know about their language. They construct tentative rules based on this knowledge and apply those rules to the spelling of words. The studies presented here reveal that a child's knowledge about written words is acquired systematically, developmentally, and gradually. The acquisition process is too complex to be limited to serial learning or word memorization. We know children do learn the English spelling system. What needs more investigation, however, is how they learn the complexities of the system.

References

1. Beers, J. "High and Low Frequency Words: How First and Second Graders Spell Them and Why," paper presented at the International Reading Association Convention, Anaheim, California, May 13, 1976.
2. Beers, J., and E. Henderson. "First Grade Children's Developing Orthographic Concepts," *Research in the Teaching of English*, Fall 1977.
3. Beers, J., C. Beers, and K. Grant. "The Logic Behind Children's Concepts among First Graders," *Research in the Teaching of English*, Fall 1977.
4. Chomsky, N. "Phonology and Reading," in H. Levin and J. Williams (Eds.), *Basic Studies in Reading*. New York: Harper and Row, 1970.
5. Chomsky, N., and M. Halle. *The Sound Pattern of English*. New York: Harper and Row, 1968.
6. Furness, E. "Mispronunciations, Mistakes, and Method in Spelling," *Elementary English*, 33 (1956), 508-511.
7. Jenson, A. "Spelling Errors and the Serial Position Effect," *Journal of Educational Psychology*, 53 (1962), 105-109.
8. Read, C. "Preschool Children's Knowledge of English Phonology," *Harvard Educational Review*, 41 (1971), 1-34.
9. Read, C. "Children's Judgment of Phonetic Similarities in Relation to English Spelling," *Language Learning*, 23 (1973), 17-38.
10. Thorndike, R., and L. Lorge. *The Teacher's Word Book of 30,000 Words*. New York: Teachers College, Columbia University, 1944.

Chapter Four

Dialect and Spelling

Elizabeth F. Stever
Brearley School
New York, New York

The evidence presented in the preceding studies raises the question of whether speakers of a nonstandard dialect follow the reported sequential spelling strategies. Since it is believed that early spellings reflect the use of phonetically based strategies, it follows that these spellings may differ according to dialect in early spelling attempts. However, it seems likely that despite early differences children of varying dialects replace phonetic strategies with more sophisticated strategies in a similar way as awareness gradually shifts from the surface phonetic level to a deeper lexical level.

This paper reports the results of an experimental study designed to test the hypothesis that dialect differences do not interfere with progression through the hierarchy of spelling strategies reported by Beers (1).

Stages	*Examples*
1. no attempt or omission of vowel element	BT for bat
2. letter-name strategy	CAK for cake
3. transitional strategy showing awareness of lax vowels and the *e* marker	MAEK for make or PET for pit
4. correct form of vowel elements	

A stratified random sample of second graders in the Alexandria, Virginia, public school system was studied. The subjects were stratified according to dialect and socioeconomic status in an attempt to control two variables suspected of influencing spelling performance.

Each student's pronunciation of the spelling words was recorded. If students used one or more of the following pronunciation features, they were classified as variant English speakers while students who used none of these features were termed standard English speakers. The term variant English is used in this study to describe the specific phonological features of southern American English that vary from standard English. All speakers showed flexibility in their use of language so that the features described here varied according to social context. In casual speech, variant English speakers may use many of these features, while in reading a word list (such as the one used in this study), they may use more features of standard English. The purpose of the following description of variant English is to show its phonological relationship to standard English.

Vowel Pronunciation in Variant English
1. /ε / before nasal consonants in standard English, as in "dent," is often pronounced /I/ in variant English.
2. Glides before nasal consonants are absent in variant English so that /aI/ as in "dime" may be pronounced /ae/.
3. Vowels before liquid consonants are heightened in variant English. For example, /I/ before /l/ as in "pill" is pronounced /i/.
4. /j/ may develop medially after front vowels in variant English such that "ham" is pronounced /haejam/.
5. /I/ is often pronounced /ʊ/ before /p/ so that "drip" may be pronounced /drʊp/.

Parent occupation as assessed by the Warner, Meeker, Eells Revised Scale for Rating Occupation was the index used to determine socioeconomic status. Parental occupation correlated highly with other indices of socioeconomic status and was readily available from school records.

The test instrument was made up of eighteen low frequency words exemplifying the lax and tense forms of the front vowels *a*, *e*, and *i*. The words were randomly reordered for

Table 1
Analysis of Variance Summary Table

SOURCE	df	S.S.	M.S.	F
Dialect (A)	1	202.58	202.58	1.92
SES (B)	1	123.95	123.95	1.18
Dialect X SES (AB)	1	79.21	79.21	.75
Subject (in Dialect X SES) (S(AB))	36	3795.70	105.44	
Category (D)	5	507.11	101.42	18.41**
Category (E)	12	469.03	39.09	7.09**
Dialect X Category (AD)	5	10.92	2.18	.40
Dialect X Exemplar (in Category) (AE(D))	12	58.36	4.86	1.75
SES X Category (BD)	5	10.39	2.08	.38
SES X Exemplar (in Category) (BE(D))	12	64.51	5.38	1.93*
Dialect X SES X Category (ABD)	5	29.93	5.99	1.09
Dialect X SES X Exemplar (in Category) (ABE(D))	12	29.80	2.48	.89
Subject X Category (SD)	180	991.62	5.51	1.98
Subject X Exemplar (in Category) (SE(D))	432	1200.56	2.78	
Time (C)	4	102.19	25.55	8.02**
Dialect X Time (AC)	4	12.10	3.03	.95
SES X Time (BC)	4	47.14	11.79	3.70**
Dialect X SES X Time (ABC)	4	22.17	5.54	1.74
Subject X Time (SC)	144	458.94	3.19	
Time X Category (CD)	20	46.44	2.32	1.77*
Time X Exemplar (in Category) (CE(D))	48	65.07	1.36	1.03
Dialect X Time X Category (ACD)	20	14.93	.75	.57
Dialect X Time X Exemplar (in Category) (ACE(D))	48	46.44	.97	.74
SES X Time X Category (BCD)	20	39.16	1.96	1.49
SES X Time X Exemplar (in Category) (BCE(D))	48	72.29	1.51	1.37*
Dialect X SES X Time X Category (ABCD)	20	37.70	1.89	1.43
Dialect X SES X Time X Exemplar (in Category) (ABCE(D))	48	39.23	.82	.62
Subject X Time X Category (in Dialect X SES) (SCD(AB))	720	946.68	1.32	1.19
Residual SCE(ABD)	1728	1904.71	1.10	

* p< .05
** p< .01

the five spelling tests which were administered over a five month period. The spellings were assigned a score of 1 to 4 corresponding to the strategy level used.

Results

The results of the analysis of variance indicated that students of differing dialects do follow the same sequential spelling patterns. Consistent with earlier research findings, the students did not appear to be limited to one strategy level for each trial. Evidently there are important influences on a child's spelling of a specific word which are not subject to control nor to manipulation by the researcher.

As was hypothesized, the main effect of dialect was not significant. It appears that all children rely on the same set of early strategies in determining how to spell a word. For example, children who pronounce *pills* as /pilz/, select a vowel that they judge to be phonetically similar to tense *e* rather than the standard pronunciation of lax *i*. While their invented spelling of the word differs from that of standard English speakers, they have followed the same spelling strategy that standard English speakers follow for a tense *e* word. By taking dialect into consideration, a very consistent use of the spelling strategies was observed.

Interestingly, the main effect of low socioeconomic status was not significant. An effort was made to control this factor to test the hypothesis that low socioeconomic status retards spelling advancement. This result may have been due to flaws in the experimental design and its implementation. However, it may also be possible that an inherent language capacity exerts a greater influence on spelling advancement than do environmental factors.

Conclusions

The evidence from this and other recent studies suggests that what children do as they begin to write down language is far more complex than was previously known. Strategies used by young children do, in fact, reflect their judgments of perceived phonetic similarities. It is clear that at the primary level spelling errors correlate with dialect divergence since children are utilizing phonological cues for correspondences. However, this modification of vowel patterns is nonstandard for all young children regardless of dialect. All children appear to spell words initially according to phonetic information. Eventually they learn that vowels are spelled alike in related words, such as *please* and *pleasant*, despite the difference in the way the vowels sound. Other aspects of words are learned and the phonetic similarity is no longer salient. It appears that early modifications of standard spelling should not be regarded as errors since these nonstandard spellings reflect a temporary phase in normal language development.

This evidence discourages the use of a language arts program which is based solely upon invariant sound-symbol relationships. Learning to read does require knowledge of sounds and their symbols, but these correspondences can be different for different dialect groups. The only requirement is that a phoneme of one dialect occur predictably in the same position in the same words as a different phoneme in another dialect. Language arts programs, based on the belief that children taught standard English pronunciation will have less difficulty with spelling and reading, fail to take into account that changing children's internalized phonological systems compares to teaching them a foreign language and requires extensive drills in both auditory discrimination and pronunciation. Such an undertaking is of doubtful value when one realizes how little correlation exists between pronunciation and mature spelling and reading skills.

The most efficient language arts materials are those which allow children to relate written English to the spoken English they already command. Early encounters with words should reflect as much as possible the phonological and syntactic systems children are likely to know. One answer is to capitalize on children's own language as a source of instructional materials. Dictations by children and later stories written by the children are logical sources of early reading materials. The children's own words then are available for numerous word study activities, including the examination of spelling patterns. Such an approach enables children to see reading and spelling as a means of communicating their ideas and feelings as well as the need for learning these processes. Moreover, when children's spontaneous expressions are shown to be of value in the classroom, the children gain positive attitudes toward themselves and toward learning.

References

1. Beers, J.W. "First and Second Grade Children's Developing Othographic Concepts of Lax and Tense Vowels," doctoral dissertation, University of Virginia, 1974. *Dissertation Abstracts International,* 35, 08-A, 4972. University Microfilms No. 75-04694.
2. Brengelman, F. "Dialect and the Teaching of Spelling," *Research in the Teaching of English,* 4 (1970), 129-138.
3. Chomsky, N. "Phonology and Reading," in H. Levin and J. Williams (Eds.), *Basic Studies in Reading.* New York: Harper and Row, 1970.
4. Labov, W. *The Study of Nonstandard English.* Urbana, Illinois: National Council of Teachers of English, 1970.
5. Langer, J.H. "Nonstandard Spelling and Language Experience in Beginning Reading," *Elementary English,* 48 (1971), 951-952.
6. Read, C. "Preschool Children's Knowledge of English Phonology," *Harvard Educational Review,* 41 (1971), 1-34.
7. Read, C. "Children's Judgments of Phonetic Similarities in Relation to English Spelling," *Language Learning,* 23 (1973), 17-38.
8. Shuy, R., W.A. Wolfram, and W.K. Riley. *Urban Language Study.* Washington, D.C.: Center for Applied Linguistics, 1968.
9. Torrey, J.W. "Illiteracy in the Ghetto," *Harvard Educational Review,* 40 (1970), 253-259.
10. Venezky, R.L. "English Orthography: Its General Structure and Relation to Sound," *Reading Research Quarterly,* 2, 3 (1967), 75-105.
11. Warner, W.L. *Social Class in America.* New York: Harper and Row, 1960.
12. Wise, C.M. *Introduction to Phonetics.* Englewood Cliffs, New Jersey: Prentice-Hall, 1957.
13. Wolfram, W., and R. W. Fasold. *Social Dialects in American English.* Englewood Cliffs, New Jersey: Prentice-Hall, 1974.

Chapter Five

Children's Spelling Strategies and Their Cognitive Development

Jerry Zutell
The Ohio State University

A growing research literature [particularly Read (*21*), Beers and Henderson (*3*), Beers, Chapter Three and Henderson, Chapter Twelve of this volume], has pointed to sensible and developmental patterns in young children's spellings. The present study has attempted to elaborate and extend this line of research in three ways: by examining the responses of a broader range of children—those in grades one through four—by examining their attempts at spelling more complex word patterns (see below), and by investigating the relationship between the developmental nature of children's spelling strategies and their overall intellectual maturation in terms of Piaget's model of cognitive stages. Thus, four specific hypotheses were tested through data collection and analysis:

1. The quality of children's spelling would improve as their grade level increased;
2. as the word categories become more complex, children's spelling strategies would be less sophisticated;

Adapted from Jerry Zutell, "Spelling Strategies of Primary School Children and Their Relationship to Piaget's Concept of Decentration," *Research in the Teaching of English*, 13, 1 (February 1979), 69-80. Copyright 1979 by the National Council of Teachers of English. Reprinted with permission.

3. there would be an interaction between grade level and word complexity; and
4. there would be a significant correlation between children's spelling strategies and their cognitive functioning.

In order to make the procedures and results of this study clearer for the reader and to elaborate on the rationale behind the study, it will be necessary to provide some specific background information regarding the three variables of word complexity, quality of spelling response, and Piaget's stages of cognitive development. Thus, each of these will be examined in more detail, especially as they apply to the plan and content of this study.

Word Complexity: The Nature of the Writing System

The English spelling system has long been condemned by scholars and educators as highly irregular and, thus, difficult to master. Appeals for reform (15) and attempts to teach reading using a simpler system (i.t.a.) have dotted the reading-spelling literature. Yet recent computerized and linguistic analyses (11, 24, 6) have progressively discovered more regular patterns below the surface of phoneme-grapheme (sound-letter) correspondences. Chomsky and Halle, in fact, argue that English orthography (the spelling system) appears to be a near optimal way of representing underlying meanings.

In order to understand such reasoning, a brief historical perspective may be helpful. At an early point in its history, English seems to have had a closer, simpler match between phonemes and graphemes. Since that time, the orthography or spelling system has become relatively stable, especially since the invention and widespread use of the printing press—the use of which made consistent spelling highly desirable. Contrary to popular understanding, it is the phonology or overall pronunciation system which has undergone and continues to undergo more radical changes, naturally affecting sound-letter relationships. However, since phonological changes are not random, but do follow some basic principles (26), the relationship between the phonology and the orthography, the pronunciation and writing systems, is *systematic* if not simple and direct. Furthermore, since changes in pronunciation are much less "visible" and "controllable" than changes in spelling, a stable writing system that preserves relationships in meaning at some expense to sound-letter correspondences has the advantage of allowing speakers of differing dialects and historical periods to recognize the same meanings, although their pronunciation may vary.

On the one hand, such an analysis based on generative phonology has a great deal of explanatory power. It especially makes sense in terms of the mature reader who can quickly and efficiently recognize many written words, get their meanings directly, and *then* produce the appropriate pronunciations in oral reading. On the other hand, such an explanation fails to account for the difficulties of beginners who have neither much experience with print nor a knowledge of the history of English phonology. This is particularly true for the beginning speller who must generate the printed form of a word having its pronunciation available to him. Thus, a slightly different, complementary perspective—one more akin to Venezky's analysis *(24)*—is necessary if we are to understand the relationship between word patterns and children's spellings.

From this point of view, the writing system can be analyzed in terms of a series of patterns which provide a high degree of regularity, if not simplicity. These patterns fall into four broad categories:

1. *Letter-Name-Sound Correspondences.* The alphabetic principle is, of course, an essential component of the English spelling system. However, it is important to recognize that sound-letter correspondences are not always as straightforward as they seem. Letter names and letter sounds are not always simply related. In fact, short vowel spelling patterns typically violate young children's letter-name-sound expectations! Thus, only a very few words (e.g., *me*, but not *met* or *meet*) can be spelled correctly using simplistic sounding strategies (see Beers' chapter for a comprehensive review).
2. *Structural Patterns* exist in words in which the presence of one or more letters affects the pronunciation of others. Silent letters are typically structural markers. "Silent e" and consonant doubling patterns are common examples of structural markers. Contrast, for example, the spellings and pronunciations of *hop* vs. *hope* and *hopping* vs. *hoping*.

Zutell

3. *Inflectional Patterns.* In English spelling, changes in tense, number, and part of speech are often indicated by word endings (*-ed*, for past tense, *-s* or *-es* for plural). These meaning-bearing elements are typically spelled the same even when they are pronounced differently because of different phonological environments. Contrast the different pronunciations of *-ed* marking past tense in *kissed* vs. *planned* vs. *lifted.*
4. *Derivational Patterns.* Words that are derived from the same root often retain the same spelling for the root element, although in the context of the overall word, pronunciations of though in the context of the overall word, pronunciations may change. Contrast the different pronunciations of *a* in *nation* vs. *national* or of *i* in *combine* vs. *combination* or of *c* in *medicine* vs. *medical.*

Given the hypothesis that the complexity of the pattern to be spelled would affect children's spelling strategies, the above analysis contributed to the selection of what types of word patterns children might be asked to spell. Five specific kinds of words were used: Short Vowel, Long Vowel, Past Tense, Consonant Doubling, and Derivational Pairs of Words. (For more information, see Appendix.)

Rating Children's Spellings

Since an expanding body of literature has indicated that children's misspellings are quite sensible and that there is a systematic developmental change in how children misspell words [see Read (*21*) and the chapters by Henderson and Beers in this volume], it was evident that right-wrong tabulations of children's spellings would hide the key element of qualitative change. Instead, a scale was developed which rated errors according to their quality and sophistication. The criteria for scoring incorporated those used by Beers (*2*), but this system was also modified and extended to include analysis of examples of the five different word patterns being used in the study.

More specifically, all spellings were rated on a six point scale (0-5). A 0 rating indicated an uninterpretable response, 1 a letter-name response and, at the other end, 5 indicated a correct spelling. Ratings of 2, 3, and 4 indicated different stages of awareness of the particular pattern being examined. (A full diagram of the rating system by word pattern category is available in the Appendix.)

Cognitive Stages: Piaget's Perspective

For Piaget, the critical question in developmental psychology has always been an epistemological one: How is knowledge acquired? And his model of the process of acquisition is basically biological: Learning is an adaptive function mirroring the more inclusive biological paradigm of the adjustment of the organism to its environment. Thus, the underlying invariant process remains: 1) assimilation of the new to the old, 2) accommodation of the old to the new, and 3) the achievement of a balance or equilibrium between the internal demands of the system and the constraints of external reality.

Therefore, growth is neither simply a matter of maturation nor one of absorption. It depends upon the interactions of several factors: internal maturation, the action of objects, social transmission, and equilibrium. The first three are, of themselves, insufficient to account for learning since "A whole play of regulation and of compensation is required to result in a coherence" (19). For Piaget a flexible internal regulation, "progressive equilibration," coordinates all other factors into an organized system.

Learning depends not only on the stimulus, but on the structure or system the learner has available to process it. The qualitative differences in these available structures, and in the way in which the organism is capable of dealing with physical experience, delineate the stages of cognitive development. Piaget (18) enumerates four major cognitive stages: sensorimotor, preoperational, concrete operational, and formal operational. Since in the present study we are most concerned with children's spelling strategies when many of them are making the transition from preoperational to concrete operational thinking, we will examine some of the differences in thinking that distinguish these two stages.

Preoperational children are bound by, or "center" on, the perceptual states of objects. Though they are aware that these objects may be changed from state to state, they are unable to compare them across states without centering on perceptual cues of limited value. An analysis of one of the typical tasks Piaget presents to school age children will clarify and elaborate this stage of centration-decentration. The problem chosen is the classic conservation of continuous quantity (20).

The child is presented with two glasses of equal size, equally filled with water. The water from one glass is then poured into a thinner, longer container. The preoperational child now typically judges that the thinner container has more water, since the level is higher. He "centers" on the perceptual state of the water and considers only one aspect of the problem. He "centers" on the height. If an extremely thin, elongated container is introduced, he may even successively vary the relevant dimension. He may now decide that thickness is more important and judge that the shorter, thicker glass contains more water. But he is unable to consider both aspects—higher but thinner vs. shorter but wider—simultaneously in seeking a solution. In Piaget's terms, he lacks compensation.

The operational child, on the other hand, may approach the problem from one of two different but equivalent points of view. Having the ability to combine classes (like height and width), he may judge the quantity of the water to be the same by compensating for one dimension in terms of the other. He may, on the other hand, also "decenter" from the perceptual state and mentally reenact the transformation involved. Thus he reasons that nothing has been added or taken away, or that the water can be returned to the original container and thus returned to its original height and width. Piaget calls this reversibility. Thus, the preoperational child, centering on a particular aspect or state, uses neither compensation nor reversibility in reaching a solution. The operational child, however, sees these as directly related to the solutions and utilizes one and/or the other in expressing a decision.

One of Piaget's more important discoveries was that these interstage differences follow similar patterns across various tasks and concepts (number, quantity, classification, time, and space).

In terms of the present study, it is being argued that efficient spelling requires a more specific but parallel coordination of structures or patterns. Efficient spelling, like operational thinking, requires a decentration away from strictly perceptual correspondences, in this case away from simply sound-letter relationships. Thus, testing procedures were used which examined each child's ability to decenter along seven Piagetian dimensions: perception (as measured by Elkind's

Picture Integration Test); class inclusion; and conservation of number, mass, continuous quantity, weight, and volume. (See Appendix for a fuller description of the decentration battery.)

Procedures

Given the hypotheses and working definitions of complexity, quality of response, and stage of development formulated thus far, the following procedures were planned and carried out:

1. Two 18 word spelling lists were constructed including a total of six low frequency examples of each of the five word pattern categories: Short Vowel, Long Vowel, Past Tense, Consonant Doubling, and Derivational Pairs.
2. Spelling lists were administered to 60 elementary school children, 15 each in grades one through four.
3. Two raters independently rated each spelling using the six point scale discussed above (percentage of agreement between raters was between 93 and 100 percent across the sixty spellings of each word). Each child's spelling rating for each of the six examples for each category were then totalled, giving each child an overall rating for each of the five spelling categories.
4. A battery of Piagetian tasks was constructed along the seven dimensions discussed above: Perception, Class Inclusion, Conservation of Number, Mass, Discontinuous Quantity, Weight and Volume. This battery was then administered and scored for each child.
5. The spelling data were analyzed using a two way analysis of variance for repeated measures design (*16*).
6. Factor analyses for oblique rotations were performed using the five spelling category scores and seven decentration scores for each child.

Results

The results of the analysis of variance indicated that there were significant effects for grade level and spelling pattern categories as well as a significant interaction effect between grade and category ($p < .01$ for all three). There was a general increase in scores as grade level increased, and a general decrease in ratings for each grade as word complexity increased. Furthermore, the factor analysis revealed that there were two distinct factors, one for spelling categories and one for decentration tasks, but that these factors were significantly correlated ($r = .56$, $p < .01$) even when the effects of grade level were controlled ($r = .36$, $p < .01$).

Discussion: Spelling Strategies

The results of the analysis of variance supported the three hypotheses generated about how children at different grade levels would attempt to spell different kinds of words. First, as the grade level increased the children seemed to use more sophisticated spelling strategies. This tendency held across all categories. However, second grade was an exception. Not only were the spelling responses similar to first grade attempts, but the performance of the second graders on the decentration tasks was also comparable to that of the first graders. Further communication with the teacher supported the suspicion that this class was, in fact, an academically below average second grade. But these children's consistent performances on both spelling and cognitive tasks tend to confirm the hypothesis that level of spelling strategy and cognitive development are significantly related.

The results of the analysis also supported the hypothesis that, across all four grades, differences in categories would lead to differences in performance. The Short and Long Vowel categories seemed of comparable difficulty, while the Past Tense and Consonant Doubling categories were also equally difficult, though noticeably more difficult than the first two categories. Finally, the Derivational Pairs category was clearly more difficult than the other four.

The children in this study seemed to rely on three different strategies in spelling short vowels. First grade attempts were about equally divided between a closest long vowel strategy and a correct short vowel strategy, with a lower but fair number of transitional attempts. This supported the findings of recent investigations (2, 3, 21, 22). Furthermore, second, third, and fourth grade spellings indicated a progressive decrease in nearest vowel strategies (minimal by third grade). Transitional attempts, on the other hand, were much slower to disappear, showing even slight increases in grades two and three. Through all the grades, the most prevalent strategies involved using the correct vowel, with almost perfect use of the proper short vowel by grade four. These findings were not unexpected. Since the children were tested toward the very end of the school year, even the first graders had the benefit of a year's instruction and a year's experience with written words. Furthermore, short vowels are traditionally dealt with during the first year of school. What is essential to the theoretical basis of this study, is that the children did employ systematic ways of spelling the short vowels, and that more of the spellings conformed to the standard orthographic representation as familiarity and maturity increased.

Long vowel spellings showed a movement from a letter-name strategy to a mastery of the marking system which structures the spelling of the English Long vowels (SKRAP—*scrape*). The first graders seemed unaware of this system, with 60 percent of their attempts being categorized as letter-name. Of the classifiable attempts of the second grade pupils, a much higher proportion showed evidence of a working knowledge of marking principles. Third and fourth graders, as expected, performed extremely well on these words, with over 90 percent of the fourth grade spellings using at least possible vowel marking patterns.

But a use of letter-name strategy did persist into the third grade (17 occurrences, SKED—*skid*). Furthermore, there was no strong evidence for any transitional stages. It seemed that when the marking system was used in the spelling responses, it was handled correctly in all grades. It may be that this finding was due to the immaturity of the second grade sample, and that an average second grade would have provided responses in which transitional strategies were used. But it is also possible that the ability to integrate both the marking system and phonetic principles was more cognitively demanding than mastering either system separately. Thus knowledge of marking principles might have been masked by an inability to use both systems simultaneously. There is not enough evidence at this time to warrant a final statement on this point.

The next two categories, Past Tense and Consonant Doubling, were characterized by a high proportion of 0 responses in both grades one and two. However, most of these unclassifiable attempts did follow a discernible pattern—spelling of the base word with the inflectional ending completely omitted (STAB—*stabbed*). But there may be a reasonable phonological explanation for this phenomenon.

As many linguists (*26, 27*) have noted, a certain amount of consonant cluster reduction is typical in the pronunciation of standard English. (This feature has also received considerable attention in recent studies of social dialects.) Consonant reduction refers to the deletion of a stop consonant (*t, d, p,* or *k*) when it follows another consonant at the end of a word. It is important to realize that in many words when the base form ends in a consonant the addition of *-ed* usually results in a consonant cluster. Thus *raked* and *trimmed* are pronounced (reykt) and (trimd). Given this fact, it may be that many of the unclassifiable responses were in reality letter-name strategies.

For the Past Tense category, the data indicated that correct use of the marking system emerged rather abruptly at the third grade level. It seemed that once the need for the marking system was realized, its implementation developed quite rapidly. Again, the noted general immaturity of the second grade sample limits the conclusions that can be drawn on this point.

The Consonant Doubling category, on the other hand, showed a somewhat different developmental pattern in the third and fourth grades. Though the children went beyond letter-name strategies, a considerable number of third grade responses revealed an unawareness of the doubling principle (HUMING—*humming*), while at the same time a smaller but still significant number of attempts showed an overextension of the principle. For the fourth grade, awareness of the doubling principle had increased, while overgeneralization remained at about the same level. The difference in the two classes also was reflected in the increased number of correct attempts by the fourth graders. Once more the developmental pattern can be reasonably explained in terms of two factors: an increased familiarity with the kinds of words under consideration and the creation and testing of a set of underlying rules. The number of overgeneralization responses for Consonant Doubling supports this contention.

The Derivational Pairs scores indicated that this category was definitely the most difficult. Once again, a high proportion of first and second grade scores were unclassifiable. An examination of the responses revealed younger children often left out whole syllables and blocks of letters, usually at the point of most interest, around the unaccented syllable of the second word in the pair. Unfamiliarity with polysyllabic words was most likely a cause of such responses. However, it is also possible that letter-name strategies were affected by constraints on short term memory. If the children attempted to move across the word in a letter-name fashion, the increased time needed to process the longer words may have led to a short term memory overload for the younger children. As a result, the phonetically least prominent parts of these words, the unaccented syllables, were omitted from the spelling attempts.

The letter-name strategies of first and second grade children were characterized by the omission of the schwa vowel from the unaccented syllable (for example, *combnashon* for *combination*). Very few of the responses for these children went beyond a simple letter-name approach.

Third and fourth grade responses, on the other hand, showed a much more consistent use of a vowel in the unaccented syllable. However, a substantial number of third and fourth grade attempts were also based on a letter-name strategy. Furthermore, only 12 percent of the third grade responses and only 40 percent of the fourth grade attempts showed the use of the same vowel in both accented and unaccented positions. For the fourth graders, the great majority of these were correct spellings. It would seem once again that familiarity and experience were factors in the way the children approached the spellings of these words. But the attempts also seemed to involve growing concepts of how words work. The principles of root word relationships, demanding generalizations and the creation of structures over classes of related words, seem to require a highly sophisticated understanding of the way words are related. Apparently these principles are mastered sometime beyond the fourth grade level.

In summary, the spelling data from this investigation generally support the argument that children progressively develop more sophisticated strategies for dealing with English orthography. However, the transitional stages for Long Vowel and Past Tense categories discovered in earlier research were not noted in the present study. Several possible explanations for this fact were suggested, but the immaturity of the second grade sample limited the applicability of the present data, especially in regard to transitional stages.

Discussion: Spelling and Decentration

The results of the two-factor analyses confirmed the investigator's original general hypothesis that performance on the decentration battery and levels of spelling strategies for each category would be significantly correlated. The fit of the two-factor solution indicated that these two sets of variables did, indeed, measure different things, but the correlation between the two factors confirmed that decentration and levels of spelling strategies were significantly related.

The purpose of the second factor analysis, using the partial correlations generated when grade was controlled, was to minimize that part of the variance predictable by between-grade differences, both maturational and experiential. The findings were that the factor pattern remained essentially the same, and that the two factors were still significantly correlated. This provides empirical data supporting the argument that the structures needed to deal effectively with English orthography are somewhat similar to the structures that must be invented in order for a child to move from preoperational to operational thinking.

Two specific sets of intercorrelations seem especially interesting. The particularly high correlations between the first and easiest spelling category, the Short Vowel category, and the decentration variables suggest that the qualitative difference between preoperational and operational thinking is most important for spelling at that time when the child first moves from a letter-name strategy to more abstractly based relational structures. Because of the effects of the Great Vowel Shift on the English sound-spelling system, a true understanding of the short vowel spellings necessarily involves a transformational system that goes beyond the merely perceptual relationships evident in letter-name spellings. More difficult spelling category strategies, though probably facilitated by more stable concrete operational thinking, did not seem quite as directly related to cognitive development.

The second interesting correlation was the significant relationship in both factor analyses between the Picture Integration Test and Derivational Pairs. Both variables specifically dealt with perceptual relationships between parts and wholes. It may very well be that the ability to internalize the relationship between *combine* and *combination* requires the same kind of active, systematic perceptual exploration necessary for success on Elkind's part-whole test.

Conclusions and Implications

Considering the developing quality of children's spelling mistakes through the grade levels tested and the significant correlations between spelling and cognitive factors in both factor analyses, it seems reasonable to conclude that learning to spell is not simply a matter of enough drill work and/or rote memorization. The development of spelling proficiency seems to involve both cognitive and linguistic processes and, as such, it requires the active, exploring participation of the learner.

Since children's spellings do exhibit stage-like characteristics, it follows that teachers could acquire useful instructional information regarding stage of development, sources of difficulty, and signs of progress by examining the quality of children's spelling attempts as well as by simply determining their correctness.

Furthermore, classroom practices like extensive phonics drills and the typical weekly spelling list-test cycle hardly encourage essential active participation and concept formation. It would seem more profitable to construct learning environments in which children have the opportunity to formulate, test, and evaluate their own hypotheses about the orthography. Such environments might logically include activities which encourage and stimulate natural language use through extensive speaking, reading, and writing as means of communication and expression.

Children also need opportunities to compare and contrast words on a variety of levels (sound, structure, syntax, semantics) so that they might systematically discover and utilize both intraword and interword patterns of organization. Activities that foster such comparisons need not be especially complicated or time consuming. Henderson (*14*) briefly suggests a word sorting procedure in which the child sorts or piles word-bank words under examples of useful classifications. It may be helpful for children to see the relationship between the spelling of past tense (typically *ed*) and its various but systematic pronunciations. Children may be asked to classify their -*ed* words as more like *raked, cheated*, or *played*.

(Of course there will be some exceptions, and other examples may be thought of as the child proceeds with the activity.)

Dale (8) and O'Rourke (17) describe the technique of "word webbing" as another activity through which older children may discover word patterns and relationships. In a root web, for instance, words like *sympathy, pathetic*, and *pathology* are linked through their common root *path-*, from *pathos* (suffer). By constructing such webs and checking their accuracy, students can simultaneously extend both their spelling and vocabulary growth through the discovery of underlying, systematic patterns of meaning and spelling.

In effect, children need the opportunity and encouragement to *discover* for themselves the structures governing English spelling, just as they *invent* (in Piaget's terms) the structures which enable them to assimilate reality, and tacitly *construct* the transformational rules which govern the structure of spoken and written language.

Appendix (Chapter Five)

List of Examples

Short Vowels

a:	craft	(21)*	*e:*	hem	(14)	*i:*	drift	(36)
	damp	(27)		speck	(13)		skid	(3)

Long Vowels

a:	tame	(25)	*e:*	creep	(36)	*i:*	spike	(5)
	scrape	(18)		thief	(28)		slime	(4)

Past Tense

/t/:	cramped	(8)	/d/:	bragged	(5)	/Id/:	dented	(3)
	raked	(13)		stabbed	(9)		cheated	(18)

Consonant Doubling

Short vowels:	humming	(20)	Long vowels:	wading	(15)
	trimmed	(42)		striped	(7)
	flopped	(5)		dining	(A)

Derivational Pairs

a:	inflame	(7)	*e:*	compete	(11)
	inflammation	(2)		competition	(28)
	explain	(AA)		repeat	(A)
	explanation	(31)		repetition	(10)
i:	combine	(A)			
	combination	(40)			
	inspire	(32)			
	inspiration	(18)			

*Numbers in parentheses are the occurrences of the word or its uninflected per million words in the Thorndike and Lorge (21) overall count. *A* indicates a word occurs between 50 and 99 times per million words. *AA* indicates a word occurs 100 or more times per million words.

Decentration Tasks: Procedures

1. *Conservation of Mass*
   Equipment—Playdoh, screen
   Procedure. Use the Playdoh to make two balls of equal size. Show these to the children and make sure they agree that both balls have the same amount of Playdoh. If the children do not agree, adjust the sizes of the balls until they consider them equal. Put one ball behind the screen and leave the other in front of the children. Roll the ball into a sausage in front of the children. Now ask the children if the same ball you rolled into the sausage still has the same amount, or it has more or less than it did before. (It is important that you give children the three choices so that they do not base their decisions on what they think you want them to say.) Then ask them to explain their reasoning. Next, bring the other ball out from behind the screen, reminding the children that the two balls originally had the same amount of dough, and that you have neither added any dough to them nor taken any away. With both the ball and the sausage in front of them, ask the children whether the balls have the same or different amounts. Next, ask them to explain their reasons.

2. *Conservation of Number*
   Equipment—Eight plastic poker chips of one color and eight of another color, screen
   Procedure. Assemble the chips into two differently colored lines of the same length. Show these to the children and have them agree that both lines contain the same amount by counting the number of chips in each line. Now place the screen between the two rows so that only one row can be seen. Change the length of the row seen by moving the chips farther apart. Now ask the children if that row has less, more, or the same as it did before. Then ask the children to explain their reasoning. Next remove the screen, reminding the children that the rows were originally the same, and that you have neither added nor taken away any chips. Now ask the children whether one row has more or less than the other or whether they both have the same amount. Ask the children to explain their reasoning.

3. *Conservation of Continuous Quantity*
   Equipment—Two identical clear plastic cups, one differently shaped cup, water, screen
   Procedure. The procedure is almost identical to that used for the conservation of mass. Now the shape of the material is determined by the shape of the container rather than by the tester's manipulation of solid material.

4. *Conservation of Weight*
   Equipment—Playdoh, screen
   Procedure. Same as for conservation of mass, except that decisions are made in regard to the weight of the Playdoh rather than in regard to its mass. Thus, a child may hold a ball in each hand in order to agree that they weigh the same. However, once the shape of the ball is changed, the child should not be allowed to weigh the objects again. Judgment should be based on what the child thinks should be true rather than on the actual physical sensation of the Playdoh.

5. *Class Inclusion I*
    Equipment—Paper triangles and squares (there should be more of
        one than the other), box
    Procedure. Show the children the squares and triangles. They
    must understand that they are *all* paper and must also agree that
    there are more of one than the other. Now ask the children whether
    there are more square (or triangle) things or more paper things. Ask
    the children to explain their reasoning.

6. *Conservation of Volume*
    Equipment—Two beakers equally filled with water (about half-
        way), two equal balls of Playdoh, screen
    Procedure. Again, basically the same as conservation of mass.
    Now the judgments are made on the change in the level of water in
    the cups if the Playdoh were put in the water. Again, however, the
    Playdoh should *not* be put in the water. The decisions should be
    made on what the children think should happen rather than on the
    physical perception.

7. *Class Inclusion II*
    Equipment—Plastic poker chips, two different colors (there should
        be more of one than the other)
    Procedure. Same as class inclusion I. Now ask the children if
    there are more of the greater number colored chips or more plastic
    chips. Ask them to explain their reasoning.

Scoring Criteria
    On the conservation problems, there are two questions—one
based on the change in an object itself (identity) and one based on the
change in relation to a similar object (equivalence). These two should
be marked *yes* if the child makes the correct judgment. Under each,
however, is a category for the child's reasoning. As much as possible
of the child's explanation should be recorded, and the reasoning
category should be marked *yes* only if the child's reasoning is directly
related to the question, and only if it makes sense. It should be based
on logic rather than on the specific perceptual situation. Thus, a
response like "they look like they're about the same" is not acceptable,
though the tester may wish to ask for a further explanation. Correct
responses are usually based on one of two principles: compensation or
reversibility. An example of compensation would be, "Now it's longer
but thinner" while reversibility is dependent on the child's ability to
see that one could return it to the former state: "If you squished it back
together, it would be the same as before." In any case, testers should be
careful that their decisions are based on what the child understands,
rather than simply on the correct verbal response.

Table 1
Spelling Strategy Rating Scale

Category	Strategy	Score	Examples of Children's Spellings
Short Vowel	unclassifiable	0	krof (craft), scod (skid)
	vowel omitted	1	krft, scd
	closest tense vowel	2	crift, sced
	transitional	3	creft, scad
	vowel correct, incorrect form	4	kraf, scid
	correct form	5	craft, skid
Long Vowel	unclassifiable	0	crop (creep), slom (slime)
	letter-name	1	crep, slim
	transitional	2	crip, slam
	vowel correct, marking incorrect	3	creyp, sliym
	vowel correctly marked, incorrect form	4	creap, sime
	correct form	5	creep, slime
Past Tense	unclassifiable	0	rake (raked), cet (cheated)
	letter-name	1	rakt, chetd
	d-marker	2	rakd, cheatd
	vowel (not e, not o) +d	3	racid, cheatud
	marker correct, incorrect form	4	raced, cheeted
	correct form	5	raked, cheated
Consonant Doubling	unclassifiable	0	flop (flopped), wad (wading)
	letter-name	1	flpt, wadn
	lax, undoubled	2	floped
	tense, doubled	3	wadding
	doubling correct, incorrect form	4	floppid, weding
	correct form	5	flopped, wading
Derivational Pairs	unclassifiable	0	xpln-xplntn (explain-explanation)
	letter-name	1	xplan-xplnashon
	vowel present, unextended	2	explain-explinashon
	vowel incorrectly extended	3	explain-explaination
	vowel correctly extended, incorrect form	4	explain- xplanashon
	correct form	5	explain-explanation

Table 2
Partial Correlations of Decentration and Spelling Variables (Grade Controlled)

	1	2	3	4	5	6	7	8	9	10	11	12
1. Number												
2. Mass	.19											
3. Cont. Quant.	.57**	.55**										
4. Weight	.46**	.56**	.72**									
5. Volume	.27*	.44**	.37**	.46**								
6. Class Incl.	.30**	.42**	.42**	.29*	.26*							
7. P.I.T.	.20	.41**	.45**	.25*	.23*	.45**						
8. Short Vowel	.27*	.40**	.47**	.42**	.13	.11	.27*					
9. Long Vowel	.28*	.07	.32**	.13	.19	.09	.04	.60**				
10. Past Tense	.15	.15	.38**	.29*	.22*	.21*	.20	.60**	.58**			
11. Doubling	.11	.24*	.34**	.29*	.18	.17	.23*	.72**	.56**	.70**		
12. Derivational Pairs	.03	.22*	.31**	.19	.20	.18	.32**	.54**	.39**	.54**	.65**	

*p<.05
**p<.01

Table 3

Intercorrelations of Decentration and Spelling Variables

	1	2	3	4	5	6	7	8	9	10	11	12
1. Number												
2. Mass	.30**											
3. Cont. Quant.	.61**	.61**										
4. Weight	.53**	.62**	.75**									
5. Volume	.33**	.50**	.43**	.51**								
6. Class Incl.	.37**	.50**	.48**	.37**	.32**							
7. P.I.T.	.28*	.48**	.50**	.33**	.29*	.51**						
8. Short Vowel	.41**	.54**	.54**	.54**	.27*	.29*	.39**					
9. Long Vowel	.42**	.33**	.44**	.34**	.33**	.29*	.23*	.78**				
10. Past Tense	.35**	.40**	.47**	.45**	.35**	.38**	.35**	.78**	.80**			
11. Doubling	.31**	.44**	.45**	.45**	.32**	.35**	.37**	.85**	.78**	.86**		
12. Derivational												
Pairs	.25*	.42*	.43**	.38**	.33**	.35**	.43**	.73**	.67**	.77**	.82**	

*p<.05
**p<.01

Zutell

Table 4
Frequency Counts of Strategies by Grade and Category

	Rating	Short Vowel	Long Vowel	Past Tense	Doubling	Derivational Pairs
Grade 1	0	5	5	49	45	33
	1	3	54	20	18	43
	2	30	2	8	8	13
	3	13	4	6	0	1
	4	34	13	5	8	0
	5	5	12	2	11	0
Grade 2	0	28	23	49	53	55
	1	7	18	14	8	27
	2	13	11	5	8	4
	3	15	4	5	2	2
	4	10	13	10	13	2
	5	17	21	7	6	0
Grade 3	0	1	0	11	7	10
	1	0	17	2	2	29
	2	5	2	0	28	40
	3	20	1	0	10	7
	4	16	28	39	11	3
	5	48	42	38	32	1
Grade 4	0	0	0	6	11	7
	1	0	5	3	1	15
	2	3	2	0	11	31
	3	4	0	0	12	4
	4	18	19	24	5	8
	5	65	64	57	50	25

References
1. Almy, M., F. Chittenden, and P. Miller. *Young Children's Thinking: Studies of Some Aspects of Piaget's Theory.* New York: Teachers College Press, Columbia University, 1966.
2. Beers, J. "First and Second Grade Children's Developing Orthographic Concepts of Tense and Lax Vowels," unpublished doctoral dissertation, University of Virginia, 1974.
3. Beers, J., and E. Henderson. "A Study of Developing Orthographic Concepts among First Graders," *Research in the Teaching of English,* 11 (1977), 133-148.
4. Briggs, C., and D. Elkind. "Cognitive Development in Early Readers," *Developmental Psychology,* 9 (1973), 279-280.
5. Cahen, L., M. Craun, and S. Johnson. "Spelling Difficulty: A Survey of the Research," *Review of Educational Research,* 41 (1970), 281-301.
6. Chomsky, N. "Phonology and Reading," in H. Levin and J. Williams (Eds.), *Basic Studies in Reading.* New York: Harper and Row, 1970.
7. Chomsky, N., and M. Halle. *The Sound Pattern of English.* New York: Harper and Row, 1968.
8. Dale, E. *The Word Game: Improving Communications.* Bloomington, Indiana: Phi Delta Kappa Educational Foundation, Fastback #60, 1975.
9. Elkind, D. *Picture Integration Test* (in press).
10. Gates, A. *A List of Spelling Difficulties in 3876 Words.* New York: Teachers College Press, Columbia University, 1937.
11. Hanna, P., and others. *Phoneme Grapheme Correspondences as Cues to Spelling Improvement.* Washington, D.C.: U.S. Government Printing Office, 1966.
12. Harman, H.H. *Modern Factor Analysis.* Chicago: University of Chicago Press, 1967.
13. Heatherly, A. "Attainment of Piagetian Conservation Tasks in Relation to the Ability to Form Hypotheses as to the Probable Content of Story Material among First and Second Grade Children," unpublished doctoral dissertation, University of Virginia, 1971.
14. Henderson, E. "On Learning to Spell," presented to the Psycholinguistics and Sociolinguistics Special Interest Group, International Reading Association Annual Convention, Houston, May 1978.
15. Mazurkiewicz, A. "Toward a Spelling Reform," *Reading World,* 16, 2 (December 1976), 81-87.
16. Myers, J.L. *Fundamentals of Experimental Design.* Boston: Allyn and Bacon, 1966.
17. O'Rourke, J. *Toward a Science of Vocabulary Development.* The Hague: Mouton Press, 1974.
18. Piaget, J. *The Child and Reality: Problems of Genetic Psychology.* New York: Viking Press, 1973.
19. Piaget, J. *Psychology of Intelligence.* Totowa, New Jersey: Littlefield Adams, 1966.
20. Piaget, J., and B. Inhelder. *Psychology of the Child.* New York: Basic Books, 1969.
21. Read, C. "Preschool Children's Knowledge of English Phonology," *Harvard Educational Review,* 41 (1971), 1-34.
22. Read, C. "Children's Judgments of Phonetic Similarities in Relation to English Spelling," *Language Learning: A Journal of Applied Linguistics,* 23 (1973), 17-38.
23. Thorndike, R.L., and I. Lorge. *The Teacher's Word Book of 30,000 Words.* New York: Teachers College, Columbia University, 1944.

24. Venezky, R.L. "English Orthography: Its Graphical Structure and Its Relation to Sound," *Reading Research Quarterly,* 2 (1967), 75-105.
25. Weir, R.H., and R.L. Venezky. "Spelling-to-Sound Patterns," in K.S. Goodman (Ed.), *The Psycholinguistic Nature of the Reading Process.* Detroit: Wayne State University Press, 1968.
26. Wise, C. *Introduction to Phonetics.* Englewood Cliffs, New Jersey: Prentice-Hall, 1957.
27. Wolfram, W., and D. Christian. *Appalachian Speech.* Arlington, Virginia: Center for Applied Linguistics, 1976.
28. Wolfram, W. "Generative Phonology: A Basic Model for Reading," in R. Shuy (Ed.), *Linguistic Theory: What Can it Say about Reading?* Newark, Delaware: International Reading Association, 1977, 32-57.

Chapter Six

The Relationship of Cognitive Development to Spelling and Reading Abilities

Carol S. Beers
Virginia Commonwealth University

In the past twenty years, there has been much research generated by the ideas of cognitive psychologist Jean Piaget. One of the interesting avenues that some of these researchers have pursued has been the examination of cognitive functioning in children with varying reading abilities (*5, 6, 14*). More recent research (Zutell, Chapter Five) has also examined the cognitive functioning of children with varying spelling abilities. Indeed, a growing body of research has suggested that consideration of children's level of cognitive functioning is a necessary prerequisite to understanding the strategies children use when confronted with written language in the primary grades [see Beers, Chapter Three and Beers and Henderson (*2*)].

Elkind (*4:7*) has suggested that children cannot deal with letters on a conceptual level until they have attained the levels of thought which allow them to consider more than one dimension of the letter. According to Elkind, children must be able to grasp the concept that letters have an ordinal property (their position in the alphabet) and a cardinal property (their name), that one letter may represent different sounds, and that the same sound can be represented by more than one letter. In brief, Elkind states that the "letter is a complex logical construction that requires concrete operations for its full elaboration." Beers and Henderson's research (2) lends support to Elkind's suggestion. They found that, when attempting to spell words, first grade children would initially employ the letter names for the vowel element in the word. This strategy indicated that the children could deal with only one dimension of the letter (i.e., how the letter sounded) and not any of the letter's other dimensions.

Furth (7:6) defines further the relationship between cognitive development and written language when he states:

> In learning to read, a child must know how to match sound patterns of the spoken language and phoneme sequences transcribed as letters. The correspondence between acoustic patterns and phonemic elements is far from simple or straightforward. For the young child who knows his language very well but does not read, the phoneme "t" in the three words "tom, but, stay" is not one invariant element but rather corresponds to three different speech and auditory processes. A speech spectogram of these words would show three different patterns with no clear boundaries of phonemes. To extract the invariance of the phoneme "t" from these different experiences means to analyze and interpret sounds. Knowing how to do this is primarily a developmental process of thinking and not a mere matter of learning a piece of information and memorizing it.

This research attempted to explore whether there was a relationship between cognitive development and facility with written language. More specifically, the research was constructed to examine not only children's recognition and comprehension of written language but, also, their spelling strategies when attempting to write certain words. The rationale for this inclusion was rather straightforward. The examination of spelling strategies provides an added dimension to children's knowledge of written language, i.e., the ability to use their knowledge of letters and words when attempting to spell. Thus, three specific hypotheses were formulated:

1. There would be a significant correlation between the spelling strategies of children in second grade and their conservation performance;

2. there would be a significant correlation between the word recognition abilities of children in second grade and their conservation performance; and

3. there would be a significant correlation between the reading comprehension of children in second grade and their conservation performance.

For a more complete discussion of the term *conservation* as it relates to level of cognitive functioning, see Zutell, Chapter Five. For a more complete discussion of the identifiable spelling strategies, the reader is referred to Read (*13*), Beers and Henderson (*2*), and Beers (Chapter Three).

Procedure

In order to study these hypotheses, the following procedures were implemented.

1. A total of 116 second graders (65 boys, 51 girls) were chosen as the subjects of this study.

2. *The Concept Assessment Kit—Conservation*, Form A (*9*) was individually administered to all children. This test is a standardized test which measures conservation performance. The test consists of six subtests including conservation of number, substance, continuous quantity, weight, discontinuous quantity, and area. The test is scored not only for children's correct behavior responses but also for their explanations of the responses. Thus, a child could obtain one point for the correct response to the conservation question, "Is there as much _____ in this one as in that one or does one have more?" An additional point is scored if the child could respond to the question "Why?" by demonstrating reversibility ("I could roll the clay back into a ball"); invariant quantity ("Nothing has been added or taken away"); or compensation ("It's longer, but it's skinnier"). A total score of twelve is possible (one point for the response, one point for the explanation for each of the six subtests). The correlation coefficient between the two scorers' separate tabulations of these tests yielded r = .96.

3. The spelling word list of Beers (Chapter Three) was administered to all children. This list includes six categories of words: short *a*, short *e*, short *i*, long *a*, long *e*, and long *i* words. There were four words for each category. For each of the twenty-four words, example sentences were used to help the

children identify the word. The only deviation from Beers' list was *peak* for *streak*—a change made because of the need for a low frequency word to replace streak, which had become a high frequency word because of the then current national fad.

The words were then scored according to the four patterns of spelling strategies found by Beers and Henderson (2). Each word was rated on a four point scale (1-4). A score of one indicated an omission of the vowel, a score of four indicated a correct response. Scores of two and three represented two intermediary steps in the attainment of a correct spelling (see Appendix for a more complete example of the scoring for each category). These scores were then collapsed into the six categories. Thus, a child could obtain scores ranging from zero to sixteen for short *a, e,* and *i* words, as well as long *a, e,* and *i* words. Frequency, a variable accounted for in Beers' original study, was not considered for scoring purposes in this study. Beers (Chapter Three) found a much greater difference between high and low frequency words with first graders than with second graders. Because the subjects of this research were second graders, frequency was eliminated for scoring purposes.

4. *The Gates MacGinitie Reading Test,* Primary B, Form 1 (8) was administered to all children.

5. The Pearson product-moment correlation (15) was used to assess the relationship among the following variables: Age, sex, IQ, reading vocabulary, reading comprehension, conservation of area, conservation of number, conservation of substance, conservation of continuous quantity, conservation of weight, conservation of discontinuous quantity, total conservation performance, short *a* words, short *i* words, short *e* words, long *a* words, long *e* words, and long *i* words.

6. Stepwise multiple regression (12) was also used to determine the combination of variables which would best predict reading vocabulary and reading comprehension.

Results

The results of the Pearson product-moment correlation indicated significant relationships between conservation performance and spelling of words in the short *i* and short *a* categories (r = .224.33, p< .01). Other significant correlations were found between reading vocabulary and conservation scores (r = .26-38, p< .01). Correlations were also significant

Table 1　　　　　　　　Correlations among Age, Sex, IQ, Reading

Variables	01	02	03	04	05	06
Age	1.00	.03	-.25**	.24**	.19*	.26**
Sex		1.00	-.06	.09	.14	.12
IQ			1.00	.13	.12	.13
Reading Vocabulary				1.00	.90**	.35**
Reading Comprehension					1.00	.33**
Conservation of Area						1.00
Conservation of Number						
Conservation of Substance						
Conservation of Continuous Quantity						
Conservation of Weight						
Conservation of Discontinuous Quantity						
Total Conservation						
Short a Words						
Short e Words						
Short i Words						
Long a Words						
Long e Words						
Long i Words						

*p<.05
**p<.01

between reading comprehension scores and conservation scores (r = .23-33, p < .01).

Significant correlations existed between reading vocabulary and the spelling of words in the short i, long a, long e, and long i categories (r = .35-.46, p < .01). There were also significant correlations between reading comprehension and the spelling of words in the short a, short i, long a, long e, and long i categories (r =.21-.49, p < .01, see Table 1).

The results of the stepwise multiple regression indicated that long e words, conservation performance, and long a words were the best predictors of both reading vocabulary and reading comprehension scores (see Tables 2 and 3).

Discussion

The original purpose of this study was threefold: 1) To determine whether there was a correlation between conservation performance and spelling strategies children use; 2) to determine whether there was a relationship between word recognition abilities and conservation performance; and 3) to

Scores, Conservation Scores, and Spelling Scores

07	08	09	10	11	12	13	14	15	16	17	18
.20*	.17	.15	.19*	.17	.27**	-.10	.05	.11	.07	.06	.21*
.08	.06	.18*	.01	.07	.12	-.05	.07	.01	.26**	.07	.13
.13	.05	.01	.04	.07	.10	.03	-.11	.12	.07	.14	.04
.26**	.29**	.28**	.29**	.17	.38**	.14	.14	.35**	.39**	.46**	.36**
.23*	.24**	.23**	.27**	.09	.33**	.21*	.11	.33**	.38**	.49**	.36**
.54**	.52**	.30**	.33**	.25**	.69**	-.03	-.11	.18*	.06	.11	.04
1.00	.44**	.41**	.33**	.35**	.71**	-.12	-.01	.19*	-.03	-.08	.03
	1.00	.47**	.51**	.45**	.79**	.30**	.15	.25**	.03	.09	.11
		1.00	.42**	.37**	.70**	.04	.11	.33**	.04	.16	.19*
			1.00	.46**	.73**	.23**	.12	.26**	.03	.12	.13
				1.00	.66	.09	.02	.22**	.13	.01	.04
					1.00	.12	.05	.33**	.06	.11	.13
						1.00	.28**	.22**	.03	.30**	.18*
							1.00	.40**	.32**	.17	.19*
								1.00	.27**	.40**	.41**
									1.00	.43**	.52**
										1.00	.53**
											1.00

determine whether there was a relationship between reading comprehension and conservation performance. The results of the analyses fully supported two of the three hypotheses and partially supported the third.

Conservation was found to be related to both reading vocabulary and reading comprehension. In general, children at a higher level of cognitive development read better, not only in terms of recognizing words but also in comprehending what they read. Why this may be so may be related to the earlier premises of this study. Word recognition skills involve a knowledge of letters, sounds, and their relationships. This knowledge requires the child's ability to decenter, to recognize that a letter can represent more than one sound and that a sound can be represented by more than one letter. Children who are at a higher level of cognitive development would be able to do this more efficiently than children in preoperational thought.

Similarly, comprehension involves the ability to see relationships between words and sentences, to understand the

Table 2
Multiple Regression Summary Table for Reading Vocabulary

Variable	Multiple R	R Square	RSQ Change	F	Simple R	B	Beta
Long e Words	.458	.209	.209	29.95**	.458	1.442	.282
Total Conservation	.569	.324	.115	19.02**	.385	.783	.272
Long a Words	.605	.366	.042	7.36**	.386	1.087	.234
Age	.618	.382	.015	2.77*	.248	.318	.115

* p < .05
** p < .01

Table 3
Multiple Regression Summary Table for Reading Comprehension

Variable	Multiple R	R Square	RSQ Change	F	Simple R	B	Beta
Long e Words	.492	.242	.242	36.14*	.492	1.269	.315
Total Conservation	.566	.320	.078	12.77*	.328	.476	.211
Long a Words	.594	.353	.033	3.69*	.380	.790	.216

* p < .01

Beers

temporal order of events, and to speculate about future events. Being able to see the relationship between words and sentences is a classification process involving multiple inclusions. Understanding the temporal order of events, as well as making predictions, involves the child's awareness of both seriation and temporal relations. Those children who are at a higher level of cognitive development should be able to do this more easily than those children who are not at that same level.

Thus, it is entirely plausible for a relationship to be found between cognitive development and both reading vocabulary and reading comprehension. Both the Pearson correlational analysis and the multiple regression analysis support this position.

The finding that the short vowel categories of *a* and *i* were significantly related to conservation tasks corroborates Zutell's finding high correlations between his short vowel category and decentration variables. This finding suggests that the ability to conserve is more important when children spell the short vowel words than the long vowel words. For example, the letter-name strategy may be sufficient to spell certain long vowels correctly but it is not sufficient to spell the vowels correctly in short vowel words. Consequently, the ability to decenter (a critical prerequisite to the ability to conserve) is more seminal in understanding the way short vowel words are spelled.

Perhaps the most interesting findings are seen in the relationships between reading abilities and the long *a* and *e* categories. It is especially worthy to note that not only were there significant Pearson correlations between these variables, but that the long *a* and long *e* categories consistently contributed to the multiple correlations. This finding validates the earlier suggestion by Beers (Chapter Three) and Beers and Henderson (2) that these spelling strategies are closely related to the child's word knowledge. The child who demonstrates a facility with spelling the long vowel words also demonstrates an understanding of more complex spelling patterns (for example, a short *a* may be represented in only one way; a long *a* may be represented in many ways). The child who consistently spells long vowel words correctly probably has a greater command of word knowledge than one who does not. In this manner, strong correlations between the long vowel categories and both reading vocabulary and comprehension may be explained.

Implications

The conclusions in this study underscore the necessity for examining current reading and spelling practice in the early years. For example, some reading series currently in wide use require the first grader to master all short vowel sounds within one level. Such a requirement assumes that the mastery of short vowel sounds is a fairly mechanical learning process. The data presented here, however, suggest that the mastery of short vowel sounds is reflective of the child's level of cognitive functioning. Thus, some children may readily grasp the short vowel category while others may grope in vain for months trying to understand it. A reading program that prevents children at this level going further because of their inability to master short vowel sounds may, in fact, be thwarting these children in their attempt to master that particular skill by requiring them to become myopic in their view of words (i.e., look at the vowel sounds only). A more productive avenue, consistent with the research presented here, would be the gradual introduction of short vowel sounds over an extended period of time along with exposure to many other sources of printed material.

Second, the fact that reading was found related to conservation performance suggests the importance of considering cognitive abilities in initial reading instruction. Not all children are cognitively able to deal with the rules and generalizations that a strong phonics program would require. It seems reasonable to suggest that reading instruction with a strong decoding emphasis should be postponed until the period of concrete operations. The decoding approach to initial reading instruction may create problems in the preoperational child who is still centering and unable to understand the hierarchical classifications which such instruction requires. A reading approach that develops a strong sight vocabulary in young children may be more appropriate. With a strong sight vocabulary, a child has a greater repertoire of words to generalize to and from once phonics instruction begins.

Finally, these findings suggest that the more children know about words in general, the more able spellers they are. Thus, the practice of isolating spelling apart from reading instruction could be questioned. Reading and spelling abilities are closely related and should be dealt with in an integrated manner in the classroom. The use of weekly spelling lists to be memorized appears to be of little value unless these lists come directly from reading material which the child will be exposed to, and instructed in, throughout the week. If spelling strategies reflect word knowledge, as this research suggests, then there is a great need for an integrated language arts curriculum in the primary grades.

Appendix (Chapter Six)

Beers' Scores and Examples for Spelling Word List

Category	Strategy	Score	Example
Short a	omission of vowel	1	HT (hat)
	letter-name	2	HIT (hat)
	transitional	3	HAET, HET (hat)
	correct form	4	HAT
Short e	omission of vowel	1	STP (step)
	letter-name	2	STAP (step)
	transitional	3	STAEP (step)
	correct form	4	STEP
Short i	omission of vowel	1	LP (lip)
	letter-name	2	LEP (lip)
	transitional	3	LIAP (lip)
	correct form	4	LIP
Long a	omission of vowel	1	GTE (gate)
	letter-name	2	GAT (gate)
	transitional	3	GAETT (gate)
	correct form	4	GATE
Long e	omission of vowel	1	WK (week)
	letter-name	2	WEK (week)
	transitional	3	SEET (seat)
	correct form	4	PEAK (peak)
Long i	omission of vowel	1	RDE (ride)
	letter-name	2	RID (ride)
	transitional	3	RIEDE (ride)
	correct form	4	RIDE

References

1. Beers, J. "First and Second Grade Children's Developing Orthographic Concepts of Tense and Lax Vowels," unpublished doctoral dissertation, University of Virginia, 1974.
2. Beers, J., and E. Henderson. "First Grade Children's Developing Orthographic Concepts," *Research in the Teaching of English*, Fall 1977.
3. Briggs, C., and D. Elkind. "Cognitive Development in Early Readers," *Developmental Psychology*, 9 (1973), 279-280.
4. Elkind, D. "Cognitive Development and Reading," paper presented at the annual meeting of the International Reading Association, New Orleans, 1974.
5. Elkind, D., J. Horn, and G. Schneider. "Modified Word Recognition, Reading Achievement, and Perceptual Decentration," *Journal of Educational Psychology*, 107 (1965), 235-251.
6. Elkind, D., M. Larson, and W. Van Doorninck. "Perceptual Learning and Performance in Slow and Average Readers," *Journal of Educational Psychology*, 56 (1965), 50-56.
7. Furth, H.G., and H. Wachs. *Thinking Goes to School*. New York: Oxford University Press, 1974.
8. *Gates MacGinitie Reading Test*, Primary B, Form 1. New York: Teachers College Press, Columbia University, 1965.
9. Goldschmid, M., and P. Bentler. *Concept Assessment Kit—Conservation*. California: Educational and Industrial Testing Service, 1968.
10. Hurta, M. "The Relationship between Conservation Abilities on Selected Piagetian Tasks and Reading Ability," unpublished doctoral dissertation, University of Wisconsin, 1974.
11. Newcomer, P., and D. Hammill. "ITPA and Academic Achievement: A Survey," *Reading Teacher*, 28 (May 1975), 731-741.
12. Nie, N., D. Bent, and C. Hull. *Statistical Package for the Social Sciences*. New York: McGraw Hill, 1970.
13. Read, C. "Preschool Children's Knowledge of English Phonology," *Harvard Educational Review*, 41 (1971), 1-34.
14. Simpson, B.F. *Multiple Classification, Class Inclusion, and Reading Ability*, final report, Project #8-A-046, Grant #OEG 1-9-080046-0010, HEW, May 1972.
15. Walker, H., and J. Lev. *Statistical Inference*. New York: Henry Holt, 1953.
16. Zutell, J. "Spelling Strategies of Primary School Children and Their Relationship to Piaget's Concept of Decentration," *Research in the Teaching of English*, 13 (1979), 69-80.

Chapter Seven

Spelling, Phonology, and the Older Student
Shane Templeton
Emory University

The interplay between the spelling system of English and the phonological knowledge that individuals possess has been an intriguing area of investigation for psychologists and educators alike (*17, 20*). The question most often addressed in the research involves the degree to which knowledge of orthographic structure influences the psychological reality of words and the phonological processes that apply to them. The question is an important one for it is part of a broader concern involving the way in which individuals organize information about the vocabulary of English. In effect, there probably are limits to the amount of information about words that we can expect most of our pupils to glean from spoken language; the rest of the information may arise from an examination of orthographic structure.

In the middle and secondary school classroom, we are concerned not only with the amount but also with the quality of our pupils' exposure to intraword, orthographic structure. Before embracing specific instructional objectives, however,

Adapted from Shane Templeton, "Spelling First, Sound Later: The Relationship between Orthography and Higher Order Phonological Knowledge in Older Students," *Research in the Teaching of English*, 13, 3 (October 1979), 255-264. Copyright 1979 by the National Council of Teachers of English. Reprinted with permission.

we must have some idea about the nature of pupils' competence with regard to word structure. The investigation of the orthographic-phonological interplay offers just such a glimpse into this competence. Most of the research in this area has involved younger children; only recently has attention been directed toward the older individual (20).

Before discussing a direct investigation into the way in which orthographic and phonological knowledge interact in the older student, I would like to consider briefly the two areas with which I shall be concerned: the nature of the orthographic "beast" and the sound system to which it corresponds.

Spelling and Phonology

English orthography is often considered a highly inefficient system that fails to represent in consistent fashion the relationship between graphic symbols and phonetic expression (1, 2). In much of the professional literature, however, the tide appears to be turning (11, 12). Recent analyses have suggested that, although English spelling may be somewhat irregular when evaluated according to the criteria of strict one-to-one phoneme-grapheme correspondences, a logical system of impressive regularity emerges on a more abstract level (21, 8, 13). English spelling does manifest its fair share of inconsistencies; research undertaken within the past fifteen years, however, suggests that the spelling system generally reflects a structural consistency only partially evidenced in sound-symbol correspondences.

Apart from phonological correspondences, spelling reflects morphological, syntactical, and derivational aspects (19). This view arises in part from Chomsky and Halle's rather extensive and, from a theoretical standpoint, influential analysis of English phonology (8). Chomsky and Halle asserted that, for the speaker-reader of English, the orthography optimally reflects the semantic relationships among words as well as quite effectively predicting pronunciation. Although this assertion about "optimality" has been challenged (20), the advantages of a spelling system which does not attempt to represent all the phonetic features of a language are widely acknowledged (13). For example, an efficient orthography probably should not represent all the phonological rules that the speaker-reader automatically applies, such as the distinction between the sounds represented by the letter *s* in the words *cats* and *clubs*. The issue of an efficient orthography usually centers on adequate representation; that is, should the orthography represent distinctions that the beginning reader will make, or those of concern to the more mature reader? Actually, a good case can be made for a kind of compromised efficiency in English; the spelling system seems to reflect competencies possessed by both younger and older individuals (*18*).

In the case of phonology, most phonological rules are mastered by children by the time they begin formal schooling (*14*). Furthermore, these rules include the distinction among the pronunciations of the plural marker *s*, as in the examples cited earlier. This type of distinction may be termed "lower order" morphological knowledge (*3*) and pertains to the pronunciation of inflectional endings (such as /s/) in various contexts. These rules are *automatic*; children apply them with scarcely a second thought about what they are doing. Where older students are concerned, however, the issue may not be quite so simple.

There are some phonological rules about which more mature speakers appear to be uncertain; these higher order rules are seldom automatic (*3*). Studies have shown that many children and adults do not have a firm grasp of the rules of *vowel alternation* (*15, 20*). These rules include vowel *laxing*, where the tense (long) vowel in certain base, or root, words changes to a lax (short) vowel in derived words, as in profane-profanity. Included, also are those instances where the tense vowel in a base word is *reduced*, or changed to the *schwa* sound in a derived form, as in incl*i*ne-incl*i*nation. To a large extent, it is possible that knowledge of these higher order rules is dependent on *orthographic* knowledge. Rather than bringing phonological competence to bear on the examination of orthographic structure, the process may be reversed, and the spelling system may influence the generalization of this higher order phonological knowledge.

Many of the words that exhibit these patterns of vowel alternation occur infrequently in everyday spoken discourse (*15*). The way in which these phonological rules are applied to this body of vocabulary, then, might be based on a deductive process. For example, when an individual knows the pronunciation and the spelling of a base word and a related derived form, he/she can be cued to the pronunciation of words that follow a similar phonological pattern by the similar orthographic structure of these words. To illustrate, let us assume an individual knows the spoken and written representation of *derive* and *derivative*. He/she can then apply this knowledge in figuring out the placement of stress and the pronunciation of the second vowel in the unknown word *appelative*, which follows a similar spelling pattern (including, in this case, the same number of syllables and the same suffix as in the known derivative). A more comprehensive and productive awareness of the rules of vowel alternation, then, may arise from the examination of orthographic structure.

The issue of higher order phonological knowledge (in this case, rules of vowel alternation) may at first glance appear to be a rather arcane concern. As suggested earlier, however, the investigation of this knowledge offers a means by which we can better understand how pupils develop knowledge about words and about the complex interplay between written and spoken language.

The Study

In an attempt to determine the correspondence between knowledge of certain higher order aspects of phonology and knowledge of English spelling, I conducted a study involving good spellers in grades six, eight, and ten. I was primarily interested in this "chicken or the egg" question of whether awareness of sound patterns precedes and is necessary for knowledge of spelling patterns, or vice versa. As the preceding discussion suggests, my hunch was in favor of "spelling first."

I chose to study the pupils' awareness, as reflected in pronunciation and in spelling, of the two rules of vowel alternation that have been mentioned: vowel *laxing* and vowel *reduction*. I believed the following results would occur:
1. Among the eighth and tenth graders, an *orthographic* representation of base words would more effectively cue correct vowel alternation in derived words than would a *spoken* representation of base words.
2. Eighth and tenth grade students would evidence a higher positive relationship between knowledge of

vowel alternation and orthographic knowledge than would sixth graders.

These first two hypotheses were based on the assumption that the older students, quite simply, had been exposed more often to orthographic structure than had the younger students. In the first case, because older students are more familiar with orthographic structure, this structure should more easily engage the appropriate phonological rules than would the spoken representation. In the second case, as a consequence of increased exposure to orthographic structure, older students have had more opportunities to generalize the phonological rules than have the younger students. Thus, we should see a closer correspondence between phonological and orthographic knowledge among the older students.

3. Phonological and orthographic knowledge should be generalizable to unfamiliar words.

For those students who have a good facility with orthographic and phonological structure, there should be a transfer of this knowledge to English pseudowords, or nonsense words, that follow the same orthographic and phonological rules as do actual English words.

4. Contextual information should facilitate correct vowel alternation.

The pronunciation of many English words in isolation is ambiguous. If an individual knows the grammatical slot into which a word can fit, information is provided as to correct stress placement and vowel pronunciation. For example, *duplicate* is pronounced differently depending on whether it functions as a verb or as an adjective.

To test these hypotheses, twenty students at each grade level were randomly assigned to one of two conditions of presentation. In one condition, each student was shown a base word plus a suffix and asked to pronounce the resulting derived word. The word and suffix were then removed and the student was asked to spell the derived word. In the second presentation condition, a base word was pronounced for the student while a suffix was visually presented. The required response was the same as in the first condition; the student first pronounced and then spelled the resulting derived word. Pronunciations were recorded for later analysis.

Twenty-four words were pronounced and spelled by each student. Half of the words were English words; the other half were pseudowords. In addition, half of the words were presented in isolation, and the other half were presented together with a typed sentence in which the derived word could occur. The following diagram illustrates this design.

		Base Word	Suffix
Real Words	(Isolation)	CONTRITE	ION
	(Contextual Clue)	URBANE	ITY
		GEORGE'S _____ IMPRESSED ALL OF US.	
Pseudo- words	(Isolation)	PERCOSE	ITY
	(Contextual Clue)	DEPLONE	IC
		TED IS A _____ PERSON.	

Results

The data were subjected to a multifactor analysis of variance with repeated measurements. In addition, intercorrelations were computed among the dependent variables. The following results were obtained:

1. As hypothesized, the orthographic, or visual, presentation of a base word did significantly increase the probability of correct pronunciation of the derived words.

2. Although the correlation between vowel alternation and spelling increases across grades, this relationship was significant only at grade ten.

3. At each grade, students appeared to generalize orthographic knowledge to the pseudowords. There was no significant difference between the spelling of the real words and the spelling of the pseudowords. Phonological knowledge, however, was not generalized; correct vowel alternation was significantly greater for real words than for pseudowords.

4. At all three grades, it was found that presenting a sentence in which a derived word could occur significantly

affected correct vowel alternation. In addition, spelling performance was significantly better for words with which a sentence was presented than for words presented in isolation.

Discussion

These findings suggest some tentative conclusions concerning the relationship between phonological knowledge and orthographic knowledge. *Seeing* a base word, as opposed to hearing it, seems to provide a more direct link with the appropriate phonological rules that apply to derivatives of the base word. That this finding occurred even among tenth graders suggests the tenuous nature of knowledge of vowel alternation. If the appropriate rules were fully internalized, then *both* conditions of presentation—visual and auditory—should have equally facilitated correct pronunciation. Furthermore, the relationship between these phonological rules and print is still inexact, as suggested by the nonsignificant correlations between spelling and vowel alternation at grades six and eight. Although orthographic ability did not differ significantly across grades, the relationship between this ability and knowledge of vowel alternation was significant only at grade ten. In addition, the greater stability of orthographic knowledge over phonological knowledge is suggested by most students' ability to spell correctly most of the pseudowords, whereas the pronunciation of these words, even at grade ten, was significantly lower than for real words.

The fourth hypothesis does not appear to relate directly to the matter of phonological-orthographic correspondence. It was tested in order to provide more information about the possible determinants of phonological rules. Results affirmed an intuitive judgment made by most teachers of the structural analysis of words; that is, the application of appropriate phonological rules appears to be at least partially dependent upon syntactic information. When a more "natural" setting was provided for a derived word, it was more often pronounced correctly. Results were quite interesting concerning spelling performance in this regard. A number of possible explanations might be offered as to why visually presented syntactic information significantly affected correct spelling; it may be that more immediately available orthographic information somehow more effectively engages the orthographic mental "machinery." Whatever the case, some very interesting further research is suggested here.

It appears, then, that orthographic knowledge may be a necessary, though not entirely sufficient, condition for higher order phonological knowledge. Most individuals may master knowledge of allowable letter sequences within words, or *intraword conditional redundancies* (*10*), and appropriate structural transformations (changing certain letters when affixes are added, for example) earlier than certain phonological rules. It would then remain for an individual to deduce the rules of vowel alternation in unknown words occurring in print from known words to which these phonological rules apply. Thus, a more efficient correspondence between an individual's sound system and the orthography may be, as Chomsky (5:17) expressed it, a "late intellectual product."

Implications

We would be putting the cart before the horse if our primary objective were to facilitate the optimal phonological development of our pupils. Not that this is an undesirable objective, it is just that it is secondary to a main focus on more general word knowledge and vocabulary development. Mature readers can understand words in print that they would otherwise hesitate to pronounce. And, as has been pointed out, more unfamiliar words occur in print than in speech. In the case of lower frequency words, then, we can take advantage of what older students may be more familiar with: a *visual*, as opposed to a *spoken*, representation. Eventually, the spoken forms that correspond to the printed examples will be created. If this were the sum total of the relationship between orthographic and phonological knowledge, we would be left with an interesting conclusion of little substance. This, however, is not the case.

Since the publication of Chomsky's *Syntactic Structures* (*7*), linguists have pointed out that it is extremely difficult (if not downright impossible) to study language devoid of any reference to an underlying logic. What is true for linguists is also true for our students. We want them to become aware of the general patterns that underlie words and to realize that to learn a word does not mean one learns a single, discrete item. Rather, one subdivides and, perhaps, expands an existing *meaning* category which is represented by other words that are

Templeton

already known. We want students to realize that many of these related words may be similar in *form* to the new word. It is in this latter regard where the spelling system can be the great organizer.

Perhaps an example will best illustrate the preceding point. Students who are privy to the knowledge that spelling can represent underlying relationships may be much more likely to perceive the logical connection between *equation* and *equanimity* if they see these words in print than they would if they hear these two words. The orthography *preserves* the relationship; the spoken representation *obscures* it.

Pedagogically, it is difficult to separate spelling instruction from vocabulary instruction (*16*), for one reinforces the other. In fact, for the older student, they are two faces of the same coin—or at least they ought to be. At issue is not a radically new approach to word study but, rather, an awareness on the teacher's part of existing proposals. Our responsibility as teachers is to direct our student's attention to the structure of printed words. C. Chomsky (*5*); Dale, O'Rourke, and Bamman (*9*); and Brengelman (*4*) have suggested some specific ways of accomplishing this, and current texts in reading methodology are beginning to explore these more intriguing aspects. For starters, we can avoid the type of instruction which honors the presentation of *infant* as a fourth grade word yet postpones the introduction of *infancy* until eighth grade (*16*).

We need to be alert to every opportunity for stretching our students' existing vocabulary structures with other examples that evidence multilevel relationships. Just as primary grade teachers group words according to "families" (*hat/fat/mat; catch/match/scratch*) so, too, can middle and secondary school teachers group words that exhibit similar higher order structural characteristics. These include the words cited earlier that follow similar alternation patterns. For extra challenge, there are always teasers such as *amnesia, mnemonic,* and *Mnemosyne*, whose structural similarities are more obscure yet still can be identified and whose semantic relationships are intriguing.

Furthermore, from the time students are capable of conceptually dealing with word origins (etymology), they can be instilled with a curiosity about exploring the common lexical roots of words. Rather than appearing as an interesting but largely unproductive comment on the development of English (to which "etymology" as a classroom topic often degenerates), this emphasis can provide a fascinating and powerful tool for word analysis.

Smith (19) noted that there are differences between the strategies for efficiently handling an unknown word while reading and the strategies for intentionally expanding one's vocabulary and orthographic knowledge. It would be pedagogically unwise to assume, however, that these strategies reflect largely independent cognitive processes for the student. Writing and examining words apart from actual reading ought to facilitate the latter, and vice versa. The observation that good readers are often poor spellers does not weaken this contention; this phenomenon may simply reflect the lack on the part of such individuals of *consciously* attending to aspects of their "intuitive" knowledge of the symbolic and morphological relationships among words.

As evidenced by the subjects in the study reported here, a closer correspondence between orthography and phonology does seem to develop with age and, one might infer, from a longer exposure to written language. By bringing elements of this correspondence to a level at which they can be examined (for example, by noting morphological, syntactic, and derivational features in word structure), this correspondence can be more fully appreciated. It would follow that a central component of the transition to skilled reading ought to be the development of an awareness of the productivity of more abstract orthographic regularity.

Emphasizing the more superficial aspects of the spelling system—sound to spelling-pattern correspondences—may be a bankrupt policy where many of our students are concerned. They require more of a "handle" on the orthography. We ought to be able to provide that handle by more qualitatively directing our students' conscious attention to the written word. On the other hand, many students are able to internalize English spelling with little conscious awareness of whatever rules or generalizations they are using. It is quite possible that most of the students in the study reported here were of this type. Even for these good spellers, there is more to be learned. For the rest of our students (and perhaps ourselves), this conscious examination should not only generate spelling competency but reinforce what I have continually referred to as a qualitatively better way of examining word structure.

It is difficult to assess empirically the quality of the conceptual frameworks that underlie the written word. As this study has suggested, a productive knowledge of orthographic structure may often precede higher order phonological knowledge. Orthography, being a more stable, visually-accessible system, may thus become the basis for a logical analysis of word-level phonology and semantics. Whenever possible, instruction should capitalize on this feature of orthographic structure.

Increasingly, research in this area is providing support for a more empirically based judgment that many reading theorists and educators have held for quite some time: the more information concerning the logic of word structure to which our students are sensitive, the more sophisticated and adaptive will be their interaction with printed language.

References
1. Allred, Ruel A. *Spelling: The Application of Research Findings.* Washington, D.C.: National Education Association, 1977.
2. Baugh, Albert C. *A History of the English Language,* Second Edition. New York: Appleton-Century-Crofts, 1957.
3. Braine, Martin D.S. "The Acquisition of Language in Infant and Child," *The Learning of Language.* New York: Appleton-Century-Crofts, 1971.
4. Brengelman, Fred. "Generative Phonolgy and the Teaching of Spelling," *English Journal,* 59, 8 (November 1970), 1113-1118.
5. Chomsky, Carol. "Reading, Writing, and Phonology," *Harvard Educational Review,* 40, 2 (May 1970), 287-309.
6. Chomsky, Noam. "Phonology and Reading," in Harry Levin and Joanna P. Williams (Eds.), *Basic Studies on Reading.* New York: Basic Books, 1970, 1-18.
7. Chomsky, Noam. *Syntactic Structures.* The Hague: Mouton, 1957.
8. Chomsky, Noam, and Morris Halle. *The Sound Pattern of English.* New York: Harper and Row, 1968.
9. Dale, Edgar, Joseph O'Rourke, and Henry Bamman. *Techniques of Teaching Vocabulary.* Palo Alto, California: Field Educational Publications, 1971.
10. Gibson, Eleanor J., Henry Osser, and Anne Pick. "A Study in the Development of Grapheme-Phoneme Correspondences," *Journal of Verbal Learning and Verbal Behavior,* 2 (July 1963), 142-146.
11. Hodges, Richard E. "Theoretical Frameworks of English Orthography," *Elementary English,* 49, 7 (November 1972), 1089-1097, 1105.
12. Howard, Murray. "The Problem of Spelling," *English Journal,* 65, 8 (November 1976), 16-19.

13. Klima, Edward. "How Alphabets Might Reflect Language," in James F. Kavanagh and Ignatius Mattingly (Eds.), *Language By Ear and By Eye*. Cambridge, Massachusetts: MIT Press, 1972, 57-80.
14. Menyuk, Paula. *The Acquisition and Development of Language*. Englewood Cliffs, New Jersey: Prentice-Hall, 1971.
15. Moskowitz, Breyne A. "On the Status of Vowel Shift in English," in Timothy Moore (Ed.), *Cognitive Development and the Acquisition of Language*. New York: Academic Press, 1973, 223-257.
16. O'Rourke, Joseph. *Toward a Science of Vocabulary Development*. The Hague: Mouton, 1974.
17. Read, Charles. *Children's Categorization of Speech Sounds in English*. Research Report No. 17. Urbana, Illinois: National Council of Teachers of English, 1975.
18. Read, Charles. "What Level of Representation Do Children Expect to Find in Print?" in P. David Pearson (Ed.), *Reading: Theory, Research, and Practice*, Twenty-Sixth Yearbook of the National Reading Conference. Clemson, South Carolina: The National Reading Conference, 1977, 193-199.
19. Smith, Frank. "Phonology and Orthography, Reading and Writing," *Elementary English*, 49, 7 (November 1972), 1075-1088.
20. Steinberg, Danny. "Phonology, Reading, and Chomsky and Halle's Optimal Orthography," *Journal of Psycholinguistic Research*, 2, 3 (1973), 239-258.
21. Venezky, Richard. *The Structure of English Orthography*. The Hague: Mouton, 1970.

Chapter Eight

Beginning Readers' Concept of Word

Darrell Morris
National College of Education

Six year olds bring a sophisticated spoken language system to the first grade classroom. In learning to read, however, children must discover how elements of this internalized linguistic system are represented in writing. They must effect a match between components of their spoken language and the printed forms on the page.

Based on their work with beginning readers, Clay (2), Ehri (4), and Soderbergh (13) have suggested that what the beginning reader needs to learn first is the correspondence between spoken words and their printed correlates in text. Ehri states (4:10):

> ...if printed language receives prior analysis into sequences of abstract word units whose linguistic identities are recognized, then its spoken form becomes evident and sound values can be related to letters where there exist correspondences. This suggests that what the beginner needs to learn is how to convert graphic cues to recognizable words.

Weintraub (16) makes a similar argument:

> ...children cannot learn to recognize words if they do not understand that words are printed units...they cannot match written with spoken words if they do not understand that words are bounded by white spaces.

It should be noted that these authors do not neglect the important relationship between letters and sounds in learning to read. They simply propose that the perception of words as units in text should precede the analysis of these units into their phoneme-grapheme parts.

Relying on clinical experience, Henderson (7) addressed the issue of word awareness in a recent monograph. He posited that children gradually develop a concept of word by learning to match the words in a spoken sentence to the printed forms on the page. At first the process is halting and inexact, but as the spacing between printed words becomes meaningful to the children, their concept of word begins to stabilize and they are able to match the temporal flow of words in spoken sentence to the corresponding spatial representations in a line of print.

A longitudinal study by Clay, as cited in Weintraub (15), supports Henderson's idea of a developmental concept of word. In tracing the emergent reading behavior of 100 New Zealand first graders, Clay reported an interesting sequence through which many of the children progressed. First, the children would finger-point to each word as they read a sentence. Next, they would voice-point or read the sentence in a slow word by word fashion. Finally, as their skill increased, there would be a lighter stress on single words and phrase reading would emerge. Clay stated that the finger-pointing and voice-pointing seemed to serve an important function in that they strengthened the children's awareness of the one-to-one correspondence between written and spoken words. Thus, from a primitive stage where the children relied on a motor response (finger-pointing) to help them focus on the spoken word/written word match, concept of word evolved until it became a stable tacit property of the children's linguistic system.

In line with the theoretical perspective of Clay, Ehri, and Henderson, the present study introduced a clinical strategy for assessing beginning readers' concept of word. Concept of word tasks were devised and presented to first graders within the context of a reading lesson (learning to read a poem). These tasks provided a measure of the children's knowledge of the spoken word/written word in reading. Scores derived from the concept of word tasks were later used to address three empirical questions: 1) Do beginning readers differ in their level of concept of word attainment? 2) Is there a relationship between beginning readers' concept of word and their reading achievement? 3) Is there a relationship between beginning readers' concept of word and their ability to segment spoken words into component sounds? (Note Ehri's suggestion that children need to discover how word units are represented in text *before* they begin to analyze the letter-sound correspondences within words.)

Method
Subjects
Twenty-one first graders were randomly selected from three first grade classrooms in a Charlottesville, Virginia, elementary school. The children were tested individually at the end of the first month of school (early October).

Concept of Word Assessment
The procedure used to assess concept of word can be described as a five-step sequence:

1. The child learned to recite a four line poem with the help of picture cues and examiner support. One of the two poems used in the study is the following:

> Sam, Sam, the butcher man
> Washed his face in a frying pan
> Combed his hair with a wagon wheel
> And died with a toothache in his heel.

2. Once the child had demonstrated mastery of the spoken poem, a printed copy of the poem was revealed and the child was informed that the printed copy corresponded to the spoken verse. The examiner modeled a reading of the first line, pointing to each word and reading it aloud. Next, the second line was framed with two index cards and the child was instructed to finger-point read the line (accuracy in pointing was recorded). Finally, the child was asked to locate two target words within the same line when the examiner pronounced the words (responses were recorded). Lines three and four were read in the same manner.

3. The examiner and the child "choral read" (read together) the entire four line poem two times. As they read, the examiner pointed to each word as it was pronounced.

4. After the choral reading was completed, the examiner pointed to individual words within the poem and the child was asked to pronounce the words (see underlined words in poem).

5. The printed copy of the poem was removed, and the child was presented with a list of six isolated words taken from the poem. The words were presented one at a time and the child was asked to pronounce each word.

This five-step sequence provided four measures of a child's concept of word: 1) ability to point to words as one reads aloud, 2) ability to recognize individual words within a single line, 3) ability to recognize individual words within the whole four line poem, and 4) ability to learn sight words from the short reading experience (step 5). An assumption was made that each of these measures was to some degree tapping a child's concept of word. The ability to point to words as one reads, to identify individual words in the context of a poem, and to obtain sight words from a brief reading experience must rest on some underlying knowledge of how spoken words are represented in printed text. Therefore, all four measures were combined to yield a composite concept of word score for each child. (Note: Children brought with them to the test experience pretests which had been administered to control for sight vocabulary.)

Phoneme Segmentation Assessment

Phoneme segmentation, the ability to segment spoken words into their component sounds (*said* = /s/ / ɛ / /d/), has been found to be significantly related to reading acquisition (*10*). The present study assessed children's phoneme segmentation ability in two ways: 1) performance on a phoneme segmentation test (*10*) and 2) ability to represent consonant segments in invented spellings (see Chapter Nine).

Assessment of Reading Achievement

Two months following the concept of word and phoneme segmentation testing, a word recognition test was administered to the children to obtain a rough measure of their progress in learning to read. Twenty-five first grade words were randomly selected from the basal reading series used in the school. Each of the twenty-five words was presented in isolation and the children's attempts to pronounce the words were recorded.

Results

Question 1

Do beginning readers differ in their level of concept of word attainment?

Table 1 shows the raw scores attained by each child on the concept of word test. The scores are rank ordered from highest to lowest. There is a considerable spread of scores within the possible response range (0-32) indicating that beginning readers do differ in their level of concept of word attainment. Clinical observations supported this finding; several children demonstrated little or no awareness of word units within the experimental poem, while others performed at a near perfect level on each of the four concept of word measures.

Table 1

Number of Correct Responses on Concept of Word Test (October), Phoneme Segmentation Test (October), and Word Recognition Test (December)

Subject	Concept of Word	Phoneme Segmentation*	Word Recognition
1	29		23
2	28	(6)	19
3	28	(6)	21
4	27	(6)	25
5	25		21
6	24	(6)	23
7	24		13
8	23	(6)	22
9	23	(6)	24
10	23		14
11	21	(6)	15
12	19		10
13	16		12
14	16		15
15	12		14
16	11		9
17	7		5
18	6		2
19	5		5
20	3		7
21	2		4

Note. Maximum Scores: Concept of Word = 32; Word Recognition Test = 25

*Number in parentheses indicates that subject made six correct responses in a row.

Question 2

Is there a relationship between beginning readers' concept of word and their reading achievement?

A Pearson Product-Moment correlation analysis indicated the existence of a significant relationship between children's concept of word in October and their December reading achievement, $r = .89$ ($p < .01$). The partial correlation, with intelligence controlled, was .87 ($p < .01$). The raw scores from which this correlation was derived are shown in Table 1.

Question 3

Is there a relationship between beginning readers' concept of word and their ability to segment spoken words into component sounds?

Correlational analysis revealed a significant relationship between children's concept of word and their performance on a phoneme segmentation test, $r = .72$ ($p < .01$). If we use a mastery criterion of six correct responses in a row on the phoneme segmentation test (*10*), there is another way to compare concept of word attainment and phoneme segmentation ability. Table 1 shows that only 7 of the 19 children who took the phoneme segmentation test in October made six correct responses in a row. Moreover, all seven of these children were found among the top 11 (out of 21) scorers on the concept of word task. No child who scored in the bottom 50 percent on concept of word attainment was able to phonetically segment words at the preestablished criterion level.

Correlational analysis also indicated a significant relationship between concept of word and a second phoneme segmentation measure, i.e., children's ability to represent consonant segments in their invented spellings, $r = .63$ ($p < .01$).

Discussion

The empirical findings suggest that concept of word, as defined in this study, is an important variable deserving of careful consideration in the analysis of prereading or reading readiness skill. The concept of word measure was found to be significantly related to beginning reading achievement and to a language skill (phoneme segmentation) which many authorities believe to be an important prerequisite to reading acquisition. Given these findings, it is important to consider in some detail methodological issues pertaining to the assessment of children's concept of word.

Methodological Issues

Over the past decade, statements concerning the importance of concept of word and attempts to assess this prereading ability have been well documented in the research literature (4). Warren (14), however, has recently noted that this concept of word literature lacks conceptual clarity and methodological agreement, and also yields inconclusive empirical findings. In his dissertation, Warren demonstrates that six concept of word tests, previously reported in the literature, differ significantly in their ability to predict first grade reading achievement.

Since an integral part of the present study was the specific methodology used to assess beginning reader's concept of word, one might well ask why one would introduce yet another procedure to assess concept of word when the complexity of this language ability has defied previous attempts to establish a reliable measure. At this point, it seems important to review some of the advantages of the concept of word assessment procedure introduced in this study and to compare the present procedure with concept of word methodologies used in previous research.

1. In the present study, concept of word measures were obtained in a naturalistic learning to read situation. The first grade subjects learned to recite an engaging four-line rhyme before they were asked to read the rhyme in its written form and to point to printed words found within it. Not only was this task purposeful and interesting to the children but, unlike previous techniques, it also closely paralleled specific reading experiences that first graders often have in the first few months of school (e.g., reading back a dictated experience story or rereading a previously memorized story from a basal reader). Psychometric considerations aside, the very nature of this concept of word assessment has immediate generalizability to the learning to read process as it occurs in the real world.

2. The concept of word tasks allowed the children to use both their spoken *and* written knowledge of wordness in attempting to identify individual words within lines of print. Previous research has focused on only one modality (visual *or*

aural) in assessing children's concept of word even though it is quite apparent that children use both aural and visual cues in learning to read. In the present study, however, concept of word assessment was specifically concerned with children's knowledge of the spoken word/written word match, i.e., their ability to simultaneously coordinate aural and visual (printed) cues in reading a line of text. Thus, we have a measure which conforms closely to the reading acquisition process and one which also meets Warren's definition of concept of word—a multifaceted ability sensitive to the context in which it is demonstrated.

3. Previous concept of word studies have examined children's metalinguistic knowledge of wordness, e.g., their ability to comment on and make conscious judgments about structural units in the language. Examples of metalinguistic tasks of word knowledge are laying down chips to mark off spoken word boundaries in a sentence (8) or drawing circles around word units in a printed sentence (12). Unfortunately, beginning readers often lack explicit awareness of word units in their language and, therefore, metalinguistic measures of concept of word are not always good predictors of early reading achievement (14).

In his review of *Psychology of Reading*, Coltheart (3:159) addressed the issue of metalinguistic (explicit) awareness in beginning reading:

> In studying language development, or learning to read, or skilled reading, it is the listener-reader's tacit knowledge which is of primary importance, since the fundamental processes involved in speaking and reading, and the store of knowledge drawn upon by these processes, *may not be accessible to introspection, and so may not be explicitly known by the listener-reader* [emphasis added].

Coltheart notes that while beginning readers may possess some tacit knowledge of the reading process, this knowledge may not be accessible to the children in tasks requiring introspective, metalinguistic judgments. Later in the same review, Coltheart suggests a way to avoid this metalinguistic awareness trap in language research:

> If one is interested in the degree to which young children are capable of making phonetic distinctions, instead of asking them such questions as "Is 'mmm' more like 'nnn' than

'shhh'?" which would only tap explicit knowledge of phonetic relationships, one can look for instances of behavior which could only occur if certain phonetic distinctions were being made (p. 161).

Since beginning readers' concept of word is the focus of the present study, we can rewrite Coltheart's methodological suggestion and simply change the variable of interest:

If one is interested in the degree to which young children are capable of making *concept of word* distinctions, instead of asking them such questions as "Is 'mmm' a word?" which would only tap explicit knowledge of wordness, one can look for instances of behavior which could only occur if certain *concept of word* distinctions were being made.

The experimental tasks in the present study reflect this search for behavioral indicators of concept of word knowledge. Such an indirect assessment strategy allows one to logically infer concept of word knowledge without requiring metalinguistic responses of the children. The novelty and importance of this approach require that we review how it works.

The assessment is indirect in that three of the four tasks which contribute to the child's concept of word score are simple word recognition tasks (pronouncing a word when it is pointed to) rather than tasks requiring judgments of linguistic structure (laying down chips to mark off spoken word boundaries). When beginning readers in the present study were able to pronounce individual words within the four-line poem as the words were pointed to by the examiner, the children were making responses which *presuppose* a concept of word. Since the children could not identify the target words until they had learned to recite the poem and been exposed to its printed form, their subsequent recognition of these words within the lines of print can be attributed to their ability to use the structure of the printed poem (the structure being letter-groups bound by spaces) to facilitate word recognition. In other words, children's success in recognizing target words within the poem indirectly revealed their knowledge of how spoken words are represented in printed text—indirectly revealed their concept of word.

In a similar vein, the children's ability to identify isolated words from the poem on a posttest also revealed concept of word knowledge. How could children learn sight words from a short, supported reading experience if they did not understand how spoken words are represented in print? They could not! And, thus, this task provided another indirect, yet sensitive index of beginning readers' concept of word.

In summarizing this discussion of methodological issues, we can cite three advantages of the concept of word assessment procedure introduced in the present study: 1) concept of word tasks are presented within the context of a purposeful, realistic reading experience; 2) the variable, concept of word, is viewed as a multifaceted ability dependent on the child's skill in coordinating aural and visual language cues; and 3) concept of word is assessed indirectly by relying on behavioral indicators of the ability. This indirect assessment circumvents the problem of metalinguistic awareness and hopefully will result in a better predictive measure of early reading achievement.

Clinical Observations

Valuable clinical information was obtained by observing the various response strategies used by individual children as they attempted the concept of word tasks.

Confusing letters and words. When asked to pronounce a given word, in isolation or context, many of the children responded by naming or sounding a letter within the word. When presented with the word *stop*, one boy responded with "sss" and, for the word *Sam*, his response was "mmm." A little girl had a different but related concept of wordness. When shown the word *pie*, she said, "Oh, that starts with somebody's name in my class." The examiner's initial puzzlement was quickly arrested by her response for the word *green*; "That starts with my brother's name." (Her brother's name was George.)

Possibly the most interesting example illustrating letter-word confusion was the response of yet another little boy. When the examiner pointed to the word *heel*, and asked the child to name the word, the boy responded by pointing to the last letter in the word and saying, "That's a one." Later when this same child was asked to pronounce individual words within the poem, he patiently explained to the examiner, "If you'll point to the letters, I'll know what you mean."

Using text structure to identify words. A consistent strategy used by most of the children in the study was to use the structure of the printed poem as an aid in recognizing individual words. For example, if the examiner pointed to the fourth word in the poem's third line indicating that the word was to be pronounced, some children would go back to the first word in the third line and begin reading the line aloud, pointing to (or counting off) each word until the target word was reached and its pronunciation could be offered. Other children went all the way back to the first word in the poem and reread the entire poem up to the fourth word in the third line.

Not all the children had to use the strategy cited above, and the ones who did apparently had not learned the target words as immediately recognizable "sight" words; i.e., they were dependent on contextual cues for word recognition. Nonetheless, the very ability to use context in this manner, to accurately count word units in a sequential order, presupposes concept of word knowledge. Children who were able to go through this behavioral sequence had to possess some knowledge of how spoken words are represented in printed text. Thus we see that the indirect, somewhat abstract assessment strategy described earlier in this chapter became a concrete and observable reality in the testing situation.

Flexibility in matching spoken words with their printed correlates. It was expected that many of the beginning readers would find it difficult to point to the individual words as they read aloud a line from the poem. This, of course, turned out to be true. However, certain words presented more pointing problems to the children than did others, and certain children were more successful in dealing with these "problem" words.

Each experimental poem contained only three words that consisted of more than one syllable (Poem 1: *gonna, away, alligator*; Poem 2: *frying, wagon*, and *toothache*). It was these multisyllable words that confused many of the children as they attempted to finger-point read the poem. For example, a line from one poem was "Give away the green grass, give away the sky." A typical reading of this line was as follows: child points to *give*, reads "give"; child points to *away*, reads "a"; child points to *the*, reads "way."

Within the clinical situation, it became obvious that syllabic characteristics of the words were causing the children to make errors in pointing. What became extremely interesting, however, was the amount of flexibility children were able to show in resolving the problem and effecting an appropriate spoken word/written word match. Some children would read right past the pointing error caused by a two-syllable word, showing little ability to correct their mistaken response. Others, however, would stop at the place of error, focus on the surrounding word units, and seemingly force the two-syllable spoken word (a/way) to fit into the single printed form (*away*). Thus, the children differed in their ability to self-correct mistaken responses while reading the lines of the poem.

Implications

1. Since the acquisition of concept of word is an important milestone in learning to read, the instructional environment should support beginning readers' developing awareness of words in text. A useful teaching strategy is to put the written message "in the children's ears" before requiring them to read. This aural memory support allows beginners to work *from* knowledge of a spoken language sequence *to* that sequence's graphic representation on the page.

Teachers should be familiar with specific instructional approaches and materials that provide language support and, thereby, facilitate development of concept of word. Two approaches immediately come to mind: *language experience approach* where children dictate their own experience stories and attempt to read them back with teacher support and *echo-reading of poems or pattern stories* where children "echo" the teacher's reading of short selections that possess a rhythmic, repetitive language pattern [strategy used in *Sounds of Language Readers (11)*].

2. It makes good sense to delay formal phonics instruction until beginning readers have developed a firm concept of word. How can children benefit appreciably from intensive work with isolated phonic sounds if they are not aware at some level that these sounds are part of a meaningful conceptual frame—the word? At best, phonics instruction that precedes concept of word teaches children something they could learn more easily at a later time. At worst, such instruction can induce confusion and frustration in youngsters who are struggling in printed text.

Once a concept of word is acquired, however, sensible phonic or word study may be beneficial to the beginning reader. Now the parts (letters) of the "known" whole (word) can be analyzed and orthographic and letter-sound regularities can be noted. Viewed in this manner, the formation of concept of word becomes a watershed event in the learning to read process.

3. Teachers of beginning reading can and should be sensitive to indicators of conceptual advancement in children's word knowledge. By watching closely for the early reading behaviors cited in the present study (ability to finger-point read, to locate individual words within a line of text, to obtain sight words from a brief reading experience), the teacher can acquire qualitative information regarding children's reading progress. Such qualitative information is crucial in successfully managing the fledgling reader, for it signals the teacher when to act (to intervene instructionally) and when to wait. Many beginning reading problems could be avoided if children were simply given more time in a supportive language environment to work out on their own the conceptual complexities of the writing system.

Regarding reading readiness screening, it makes little sense to continue to view readiness as a single score on a test of isolated, unrelated skills when it is possible to gain qualitative, process-related information from a brief reading experience with a child. The teacher can do this using the very procedure introduced in this study. Neither test protocols nor test norms are needed; the only requirement is a little teacher judgment based on observation of children in real reading situations.

Summation

Henderson (7) has argued persuasively that the first months of formal reading instruction represent a fragile learning period fraught with the potential for misunderstanding basic concepts. At no time during a child's education does the teacher bear a greater responsibility for providing sensitive, knowledgeable instruction.

Ironically, psychological and educational research have been able to provide teachers with little guidance in better understanding the critical period of beginning reading. Psychometric tests of "reading readiness" that yield numerical scores are of questionable value, and certainly do not provide information pertaining to the specific instructional needs of individual children. On the other hand, experimental attempts to isolate the underlying components of beginning reading skills have often been characterized by artificial, task-specific methodologies that afford little or no generalizability to the teaching enterprise.

The present study attempts, in a small way, to bridge this chasm between theory and practice. Based on a logical analysis of the initial reading task, a specific ability (concept of word) has been isolated, investigated, and found to be significantly related to reading achievement. Furthermore, the methodology used to investigate this ability can be immediately transferred from the experimental situation to the teaching situation. We are left with a conceptual (as opposed to psychometric) measure of reading readiness that has applicability in the classroom.

References

1. Clay, Marie M. "Emergent Reading Behavior," unpublished doctoral dissertation, University of Auckland, Auckland, New Zealand, 1966.
2. Clay, Marie M. "Reading Errors and Self-Correction Behavior," *British Journal of Educational Psychology*, 39 (1969), 47-56.
3. Coltheart, M. "Review of Gibson and Levin's *Psychology of Reading,*" *Quarterly Journal of Experimental Psychology,*29 (1977), 157-167.
4. Ehri, Linnea C. "Beginning Reading from a Psycholinguistic Perspective: Amalgamation of Word Identifies," in Frank Murray (Ed.), *The Recognition of Words*. Newark, Delaware: International Reading Association, 1978.
5. Gibson, E.J., and H. Levin. *The Psychology of Reading*. Cambridge, Massachusetts: MIT Press, 1975.
6. Henderson, E.H. "Some Cognitive Aspects of Learning to Spell English," paper presented to the Language Experience Special Interest Group, International Reading Association Annual Convention, Anaheim, 1976.
7. Henderson, E.H. "Forward to Basics in Reading Instruction," unpublished monograph, University of Virginia, 1977.
8. Holden, M.H., and W.H. MacGinitie. "Children's Conception of Word Boundaries in Speech and Print," *Journal of Educational Psychology*, 63 (1972), 551-557.
9. Liberman, I.Y. "Segmentation of the Spoken Word and Reading Acquisition," *Bulletin of the Orton Society*, 23 (1973), 65-67.
10. Liberman, I.Y., and others. "Explicit Syllable and Phoneme Segmentation in the Young Child," *Journal of Experimental Child Psychology*, 18 (1974), 201-212.
11. Martin, B. *Sounds of Language Readers*, Teacher's Edition. New York: Holt, Rinehart and Winston, 1966.

12. Meltzer, N.S., and R. Herse. "The Boundaries of Written Words as Seen First Graders," *Journal of Reading Behavior*, 1 (1969), 3-13.
13. Soderbergh, Ragnhild. *Reading in Early Childhood*. Washington, D.C.: Georgetown University Press, 1977.
14. Warren, B. "Children's Word Boundary Recognition Ability: Methodological Considerations," unpublished doctoral dissertation, State University of New York at Albany, 1977.
15. Weintraub, S. "Some Implications for Beginning Reading," *Reading Teacher*, 22 (1968), 63-67.
16. Weintraub, S. "What Research Says about Learning to Read," in H.M. Robinson (Ed.), *Coordinating Reading Instruction*. Glenview, Illinois: Scott, Foresman, 1971.

Chapter Nine

Three Steps to Teaching Beginning Readers to Spell

J. Richard Gentry
Western Carolina University

Edmund H. Henderson
University of Virginia

English orthography is not a system that is dominated by the surface sounds of spoken language. To learn to spell is not to get in the habit of associating sounds directly with letters. Rather, English spelling is dominated by underlying sound segments which convey meaning. Learning to spell is a matter of acquiring knowledge rather than habits—in this case, knowledge of how the alphabet reflects meaningful language.

How then may these principles be applied to teaching beginning readers to spell? For kindergarten or first and second grade teachers, we would identify three steps for becoming a better teacher of spelling, and thereby of reading and writing.

The first step is to *encourage creative writing*. Allow children to assume active roles in acquiring written language. Children must manipulate and discover words. They must test their theories of how the alphabet works by contrasting their productions with standard orthography. Children do these things when they are encouraged to write independently. Such

Adapted from *The Reading Teacher*, 31 (March 1978), 632-637.

encouragement guides them to the threshold of acquiring written language facility. Chomsky (1) has suggested that children should write first and read later. Unquestionably, kindergartners and first and second graders can produce expressive, meaningful written language. Let's look at some examples.

Jim is an average reader in the first grade. He produced this story in April.

MOIE [My] Dad ran in the MRATHON [marathon] and WEN [when] he came home he had a INGRD [injured] LEGA [leg] but it WUS [was] ONELEE [only] a WECKEGO [week ago] and he CUD [could] WOC [walk] on the THRD [third] day

The story is meaningful and well written in terms of clarity and expressiveness. Jim's teacher will type the story supplying the standard spelling and put it into the class book. When Jim and his classmates read and reread the story, they will be exposed to standard spelling, but the integrity of his original production is never questioned.

Lilia, an average first grader in an innercity school, pretends that she is an apartment building when she creates the following story.

I am a building. I have a ELEVATR [elevator] on me
A lot OV [of] PEPL [people] are on me and they work
on me
One PRSN [person] is TIPING [typing] and A NOTHR
[another] PRSN [person] is sleeping and THAR
[there] is a lot OV [of] PEPL [people] on me
I see a LADE [lady] COTTING [cutting] the GRAS
[grass] BECASE [because] she helps the building to
be open and WANE [when] I go on the ELEVATR
[elevator] it SEAS [sees] me that is the end Lilia

Lilia's writing is expressive, creative, and interesting. An analysis of Lilia's spelling reveals that she is well on the way to becoming a good writer and a proficient speller. Seventy-six percent of the words which Lilia has used in this story are spelled correctly. Analysis of her spelling choices shows good reasoning and excellent auditory discrimination. They give us an idea of what Lilia already knows about words, and an idea of the kinds of experiences with words that should help Lilia continue to progress toward a more abstract, standard spelling.

From her productions, it is evident that Lilia is testing the orthography and internalizing its rules. Her experiences with words at this early stage will undoubtedly build the framework from which she can develop into an accurate speller.

Step two for teaching beginning readers to spell is to *de-emphasize standard spelling*. In the primary grades, children must be encouraged to spell as best they can and not be held accountable for adult spelling standards.

Perhaps the suggestion that teachers do require adult standards of their beginning spellers seems a bit preposterous. On the other hand, it is not uncommon to hear teachers report that their children cannot spell or that writing should be pursued only after some standard of correct spelling can be maintained.

Parents, too, are often guilty of demanding strict spelling accuracy from beginning writers. All too frequently, children take home creative writings in which the nonstandard spellings have not been corrected. Parents rush to the phone to demand why teachers are not doing their jobs. Such confrontations can be avoided. Parents should be informed of the merits of frequent creative writing exercises and of the integrity of early spelling attempts. They should understand that a teacher may closely scrutinize nonstandard spelling and follow a child's spelling development without bringing unnecessary attention to errors.

When parents come in for a conference, they should be shown a folder where their child's independent writing has been collected. Over a period of several months it will be obvious that, through frequent writing experiences, the child is developing as a speller. This system of evaluating early spelling progress is much more satisfactory than reporting how many words a child has spelled correctly on a spelling list each Friday.

One teachers tells the following story about Parents' Night and first grade spelling. A particular little girl was showing her writing folder to her parents to point out the progress she had made in spelling. Glancing through some of her earlier writing samples, this first grader commented,

Gentry and Henderson

"Look, Mom! Isn't that spelling gross?" It was obvious that the child was pleased with her progress. The evaluation procedure was convincing to the parents, and the teacher received plenty of encouragement for continuing the vigorous creative writing program.

A primary teacher who de-emphasizes standard spelling is less concerned with correctness than with understanding the reasoning process that a child has used to arrive at a particular spelling. Of course, a child's reasoning process cannot be examined directly. But a teacher can examine a child's nonstandard spellings and infer the quality of a child's knowledge of words as well as the child's conceptualization of written language.

Three five year olds, with whom we recently have worked, are each in their eighth month of kindergarten. Monica knows all the letters of the alphabet. Tesscha knows most of the letters though she does not know *I* or *U*. James knows only nine of the letters by name though he can write some letters from memory. Each of the children has a theory of how the alphabet reflects language and proceeds with a spelling strategy based on that theory. Some of their productions are shown in Figure 1.

Figure 1
Spellings of Three Kindergartners

Word	Monica's Spelling	Tesscha's Spelling	James' Spelling
monster	MONSTR	MTR	AM1
united	UNINTID	NNT	EM3321
dressing	DRESING	JRASM	8EmaAPS
bottom	BODM	BODM	19nHM
hiked	HIKT	HOT	SAnH
human	HUMIN	HMN	MENENA

Monica employs a spelling strategy that is strictly phonetic. She corresponds the letters of the alphabet directly to the surface sound of the words she wishes to spell. Her judgments are consistent and show excellent auditory discrimination. For example, she uses the letters *id* and *t* respectively, to represent the *-ed* inflectional ending of *united* and *hiked*. These are correct phonetic representations. Monica's spelling is typical of a spelling pattern frequently found in first grade.

Tesscha has the rudiments of a phonetic system and again demonstrates good auditory discrimination. For example, *jr* is a logical phonetic choice based on the affrication of /t/ when it occurs before /r/ in English. This phonetic property, affrication, which Tesscha has represented, is perceptually correct. A limitation of Tesscha's spelling strategy is that she tends to omit certain features, particularly vowels. A teacher who observed Tesscha's spelling patterns should recognize the need to reintroduce the letters *u* and *i*. Although Tesscha's use of *o* for the /ai/ sound in *hiked* is rather unusual, she used that strategy consistently, spelling tense *i* with *o* for all such words on the spelling list. Even at this early stage, she is capable of producing abstract representations, and her spelling is remarkably systematic. Thus, she is already employing two of the basic principles of standard English orthography.

James' spelling is quite deviant and differs radically from any of the attempts produced by the other one hundred kindergartners in his school. Certainly he suffers in terms of reading readiness. James has learned only a few letters of the alphabet. His strategy for spelling appears to be a random ordering of the letters he can write. James makes some letter reversals—not an unusual occurrence for a child of his age. He also writes some words from right to left. His teacher should point out that English does not work that way. Most unusual is James' use of numbers to write words. This, more than any other facet of his nonstandard productions, is an indication of the poverty of James' knowledge of written words.

A diagnostic consideration of the spelling patterns of each of these children will enable a teacher to make some important judgments in assessing the child's reading readiness and knowledge of written language. The teacher may consider James, Tesscha, and Monica individually to determine what kinds of activities each child needs in order to make progress. Crucial pedagogical judgments such as these are based on nonstandard spellings, not on how many words a child can spell correctly.

Diagnostic Cues

After encouraging creative writing and de-emphasizing standard spelling, step three should follow quite naturally. A teacher should learn to *respond appropriately to nonstandard spelling.* Informed teachers realize that most children approach reading and writing with some prior conception of their structure. If a child is using a strict phonetic strategy, a teacher should avoid confusing her/him with an exaggerated sounding out of the word. A child who has spelled the beginning sound of *trade* with *ch* does not need to be told to listen for the sound. The child hears the sound quite clearly and is representing the phonetic feature, affrication.

What the child does need is the opportunity to manipulate words so that the relationships among spelling, meaning, and phonology become clear. An informed teacher might point out a word that the child does know that begins with the same sound—*track, tree, truck,* or *trick*. The child should be permitted to contrast these words with words that begin with *ch—Chuck, chick, church,* and *chat*. Conceding that all of these words have some similarity in beginning sounds, the informed teacher would point out that *track, tree* and *truck* also begin like *tip, tap,* and *top*. Finally, the teacher would have the child categorize the words according to their standard spelling, those that begin with *t*, those that begin with *ch*, and those with *tr*.

In order to respond appropriately to nonstandard spelling, the teacher must recognize transition from one developmental strategy to the next. In first graders, the teacher must look for the movement away from a purely phonetic strategy to a more abstract representation of what the child hears. The spellings in Figure 2 demonstrate abstracting away from phonetic variation as one follows the progression from phonetic to transitional to correct spelling strategies. Read (2:78) has observed that children "are on their way when they begin to abstract away from phonetic variation." Abstraction is a crucial step toward becoming an accurate speller.

Figure 2
Three Spelling Strategies

Phonetic	Transitional	Correct
MOSTR	MONSTOR	MONSTER
ATE	EIGTY	EIGHTY
HIKT	HICKED	HIKED
LUVATR	AELUVATER	ELEVATOR
EGL	EGGLE	EAGLE
UNIDID	YOUNIETED	UNITED

Teachers should recognize the nonstandard spellings that are predictable, frequent, and natural in the writing of beginning readers. A knowledgeable presentation of them appears in Read's monograph. Figure 3 presents four of the categories of nonstandard spelling that frequently appear in the writing of kindergartners and first and second graders. Section A provides examples in which certain lax ("short") vowels are typically replaced by others. Section B demonstrates the omission of vowels from syllables containing consonants that function as vowels, namely, *r, l, m*, and *n*. Note that again the spelling is phonetically accurate.

Figure 3
Four Common Categories of Nonstandard Spelling

	Phonetic Spelling	Phonetic Feature
A. Substitutions for lax vowels		
A for E as in *bet*	BAT	Lax E
E for I as in *sit*	SET	Lax I
I for O as in *cot*	CIT	Lax O
O for U as in *hut*	HOT	Lax U
B. Omission of vowel when syllable has a vowel-like ("syllabic") consonant		
bi*r*d	BRD	Stressed retroflex vowel
siste*r*	SISTR	Unstressed retroflex vowel
bott*l*e	BOTTL	Sonorant /l/
ope*n*	OPN	Sonorant /n/
Ada*m*	ADM	Sonorant /m/
C. Use of *D* to render the flap phoneme for *t* between vowels		
pretty	PREDE	Alveolar flap
bottom	BODM	Alveolar flap
eighty	ADE	Alveolar flap
D. Use of *T* to render /t/ in past tense form of certain verbs		
liked	LIKT	Past tense /t/
looked	LOOKT	Past tense /t/
peeked	PEKT	Past tense /t/

As shown in Section C, /t/ may be given a nonstandard spelling *d* when it occurs between vowels. This reflects clearly the American pronunciation, which substitutes a flap of the tongue tip against the upper gum ridge for /t/ in this medial position. A fourth regular nonstandard spelling, shown in Section D, is the use of *t* for the past tense *-ed* in words where the pronunciation actually is /t/.

How well do you understand the spelling of beginning readers? Try to read these examples of children's writing. Can you identify the child's spelling strategy? Do you understand why the child has spelled the word in a particular nonstandard form?

WANS a rolling roll was SMOOTING the STREETE. WHNE FINLEE the old MASHENE broke down. You will find it in a FATERE It eats OLE. It helps you by SMOOTING the STREETE.   Robby, first grade

I went to PENSLVANEUO Monday for 3 days WEN I was THAIR the LITTL GRIL had the CINCINPOCS I WASIT going to get them. BE COS I OLRETEA had them.   Joey, first grade

Spring is a time WIN EVRY BUTTY is OUTSID and I like it BE CAS it is hot and sunny! On JUN 15thth I am MOUVING.   Lisa, first grade

In conclusion, we'll reiterate the three steps for becoming a better teacher of spelling and, thereby, of reading and writing.

1. Encourage creative writing.

2. De-emphasize standard spelling.

3. Learn to respond appropriately to nonstandard spelling.

References

1. Chomsky, Carol. "Write First, Read Later," *Childhood Education*, 47 (1971), 296-299.
2. Read, Charles. *Children's Categorization of Speech Sounds in English*, Research Report No. 17. Urbana, Illinois: National Council of Teachers of English, 1975.

Chapter Ten

Words, Kids, and Categories
Jean Wallace Gillet
M. Jane Kita
University of Virginia

Categorization, grouping together different stimuli into classes based on common properties, is one of the most fundamental human cognitive activities. The ability to treat different stimuli as equivalent is intimately involved with the formation of concepts, our organized units of knowledge.

There appears to be a number of reasons why categorization serves human thinking so well. Anglin (*1*) has called categorization "a ubiquitous cognitive activity" which research indicates is involved in concept formation as well as in perception, memory, problem solving, and almost all linguistic behavior.

According to Anglin (*1*); Bruner, Goodnow, and Austin (*2*); and Piaget (*7*), categorizing objects and events allows us to create order in a world which bombards our senses with stimuli. When we recognize similarities in objects or events, we can relate them to each other and consequently create groups or categories of·similar things. In this way, new things do not remain forever unique but can be considered in relation to everything else that is already familiar.

Adapted from *The Reading Teacher*, 32 (February 1979), 538-542.

When we can classify an object (or event or idea) as being like some others, we can form generalizations about the properties of all the members of the category and use these generalizations to form hypotheses about new experiences. In short, we can use information about the environment to form expectations about how things and forces may be related. Thus we not only can make order and sense of what has been experienced but can meet new stimuli with strategies for making sense of them and with hypotheses about how they ought to behave and relate to the rest of the world.

Experts in the field of child development (3, 4, 5, 10) agree that a major aspect of children's cognitive growth is their powerful and autonomous drive to explore, experience, and make sense of their environment. From the first weeks of life, children are extremely active builders of cognitive categories. They acquire almost all their knowledge and store of concepts by interaction with people, things, events, and language rather than by imitation or passive observation (8). Children do not internalize preset categories but discover and create categories themselves, a process which seems to proceed in orderly and predictable stages (1, 5).

Categorization appears to be one of the most basic and powerful operations of human thinking, responsible for much of children's natural learning. In particular, categorization is intimately involved in language acquisition and the formation of verbal concepts (1, 5, 6).

Putting Grouping Abilities to Work

Children should be provided with opportunities to exercise and develop categorization abilities in school, particularly in instruction aimed at developing word knowledge.

In reading instruction, much time is spent helping children develop strategies for recognizing words in print and analyzing those they do not immediately recognize. We often forget that children have well developed feature analysis abilities when they begin to learn to read and that they can and do search for similarities in things, categorize them, and draw generalizations and inferences about new things which might also fit those categories. We believe we can productively put those abilities to use in the classroom.

In teaching reading, we can help children organize and extend their natural ability to discern those features that distinguish one word from others, thus expanding their understanding of how words are related. This is accomplished by systematically providing opportunities for children to study and categorize words themselves. Categorization based on feature analysis and induction enables children to recognize new words and written language structures (9).

Word Sort

A vehicle for this kind of systematic word study is the "word sort." In a word sort, a child or group of children categorizes words written on cards by physically grouping them. The features a word may have in common with others can be shared letters, similarities in letter sounds, structural elements, grammatical functions, or related meaning. All of these features are important in word recognition and word analysis.

Word sorts differ from more traditional word recognition/analysis methods in that, in sorting, children are led to discern for themselves the features words have in common, rather than being told how words are similar and being expected to remember and apply preset rules.

There are two basic types of sorts. In "closed sorts," the criterion which the words in a group must share is stated in advance of sorting; for instance, words with the same initial letter or the same vowel sound, or words derived from the same base word.

In "open sorts," no criterion is stated in advance. Rather, word groups are formed as a body of words is examined and relationships suggest themselves naturally. In closed sorts, the children search for instances of a shared feature, exercising convergent thinking and deduction; in open sorts, children consider several features simultaneously and search for those which are shared by other words, exercising divergent thinking and induction. Both types of sort are dynamic, creative word study activities which encourage children to study words critically. They are powerful tools in helping children organize what they know about words and form generalizations they can productively apply to unknown words.

How to Begin Word Sorts

As with any new activity, word sorts are most effectively introduced in small groups of eight to ten children. Initially, the word sort activity should be highly structured so that confusion over procedures is minimized.

With beginning readers, it is fruitful to start by giving the children picture cards to sort into categories. This task provides them with the experience of physically placing cards into categories based on their judgements of how things go together; for example, they could sort vegetables from fruits, or house pets from zoo animals.

Once the mechanics of sorting are established using the pictures, the teacher can initiate sorts which focus on specific word features. In the beginning stages, features related to sound are most frequent. For instance, if teachers wish to introduce the initial blends *br* and *fr*, they might begin by conducting an auditory lesson, requiring students to discriminate between these initial sounds when given pairs of words. This type of experience offers the children the opportunity to focus on the word feature in listening. Once students can successfully do this, the teacher begins the actual word sort activity in the reading circle.

In this initial closed task, the teacher sets the categories using picture cards as key words. Pictures of a broom and a frog might serve as *br/fr* category labels. Seated on the floor, each child receives a number of picture cards of objects whose names fit by initial sound into one of the two categories. A miscellaneous category should be included where children can place cards of which they are uncertain. The children then individually sort their cards into the categories designated by the key cards. At this stage it is important to use pictures rather than words, so that the children rely on an internalization of the concept of initial sound rather than on a visual matching of letters.

Once the children can easily sort the pictures into the appropriate categories, the teacher may introduce sorting with word cards. Since it is essential that children work with words they already recognize, sight words are used. Categories are again established by the teacher using picture cards as key words. The teacher distributes the word cards and the children individually sort the word cards into piles as they did with the picture cards.

As children place the cards into the categories, the teacher notes how they are sorting, and gives the students immediate feedback concerning the grouping of the cards. Information is provided about each youngster's mastery of the particular skill.

Having reached this point, the children are familiar and comfortable with the mechanics of sorting. The teacher now breaks the reading circle into smaller groups of three or four children. Word cards are distributed to each, and their task is to sort their cards into categories according to any criterion they choose. In this open sort game, "Guess My Group," each of the children receives ten word cards to sort into as many categories as possible. Once they have created their categories, students must try to guess how the others in the group have to play them on another's category, using induction to determine what the criterion may be.

This type of open sort is also a useful diagnostic tool. During the activity the teacher can observe the diverse types of sorts the children are making spontaneously. One child may sort by initial sounds, while a more advanced child may sort according to vowel sounds or number of syllables. Information like this is useful in planning future word study instruction and activities.

Word sorts can be used equally well with more advanced readers. As the children's reading ability improves and their word knowledge grows, sort activities can be used to explore vowel and spelling patterns, word meanings, etymology, and parts of speech.

Extensions: Word Sort Games

Reading circle instruction can be extended using the format of board and card games. An example is a modification of tic-tac-toe. A game board is made by dividing a piece of cardboard into nine equal sections (three by three). One word card is placed in each section. Players are given eight word cards and markers (plastic, paper, etc.). Children then take turns attempting to make a category with one of their cards and one of the cards on the board, using any word feature they find. If a child or team of children can do so successfully, a marker that identifies their team is placed on that square. Play continues until someone wins the game by placing three markers in a row diagonally, vertically, or horizontally.

A card game based on "Concentration" can be adapted to word sort activities using a deck of word cards. After the cards are shuffled, sixteen are placed face down on the table. Each player turns over two cards and attempts to sort or put the words together in some way—by beginning sound, number of syllables, or meaning. If the player can justify the sort and the others accept it, the child can pick up the two cards, then turn over two more. If on the next try a sort cannot be made, the child replaces the cards face down and another player goes through the procedure. The player who picks up the most cards is the winner.

Other card game variations can be played using the formats of "Rummy," "Fish," and "Old Maid." In each of these, rather than simply matching pairs of word cards, children categorize according to salient word features.

Word sorts are a workable alternative to traditional word study programs. In several ways, they are more advantageous. Rather than specifying the sequence of particular word features to be taught, word sort activities allow children to demonstrate what they already know, what they are learning, and what they need to learn. These categorization activities allow children to form generalizations about how words are related, using not only phonic features but the equally important relationships of structure, grammatical function, and meaning. With generalizations about these relationships, children can productively apply understanding of words to new words they encounter.

Word sorts provide an opportunity for children to teach and learn from each other while discussing and examining words together. This is a critical aspect of learning which is not present when children spend most of their word study time individually completing worksheets.

Word sorts also make economical use of teacher time and materials. There are no dittos to run off or correct. Instead, the teacher's time is spent directly teaching and diagnosing. The only materials needed are index cards.

Finally, word sort activities are flexible enough to be used with individuals and groups, with teacher direction or as independent activities. They "grow" with the children, from early prereaders to fluent mature readers; from young children's vocabularies limited by their experience with the world to the widely differentiated, precise vocabularies and word knowledge of adults.

References

1. Anglin, Jeremy M. *Word, Object, and Conceptual Development.* New York: W.W. Norton, 1977.
2. Bruner, Jerome S., Jacqueline J. Goodnow, and George A. Austin. *A Study of Thinking.* New York: John Wiley, 1966.
3. Bruner, Jerome S., Rose R. Oliver, and Patricia M. Greenfield. *Studies in Cognitive Growth.* New York: John Wiley, 1966.
4. Hunt, J.McVicker. *Intelligence and Experience.* New York: Ronald Press, 1966.
5. Inhelder, Barbel, and Jean Piaget. *The Early Growth of Logic in the Child.* New York: W.W. Norton, 1964.
6. Nelson, Katharine. "Concept, Word, and Sentence: Interrelations in Acquisition and Development," *Psychological Review,* 81, 4 (July 1974), 267-285.
7. Piaget, Jean. *The Origin of Intelligence in Children.* New York: International Universities Press, 1952.
8. Sinclair-de-Zwart, Hermine."Language Acquisition and Cognitive Development," in T.E. More (Ed.), *Cognitive Development and the Acquisition of Language.* New York: Academic Press, 1973.
9. Temple, Charles, and Jean Wallace Gillet. "Developing Word Knowledge: A Cognitive View," *Reading World,* December 1978.
10. White, Burton L. *The First Three Years of Life.* Englewood Cliffs, New Jersey: Prentice-Hall, 1975.

Chapter Eleven

Word Concept Development Activities

Elizabeth Sulzby
Northwestern University

Teachers who accept the centrality of meaning in the process of learning to read, including proponents of the language experience approach (*23*) or other whole language approaches (*13*), often feel uneasy about tasks in which words are studied in isolation. They hold that words so treated often become less than foreign objects, distorted by their isolation from meaningful text. I have no quarrel with this stance when words are, indeed, isolated as they often are in standard phonics workbooks. Reading, in my conception, is comprehending and, thus, is an important part of our attempt to make sense out of our world (*10*). While words may not be the most important or primary unit of language in comprehending, written material is composed of words. Furthermore, we name concepts in our world with words. Children find words very fascinating things to talk about and to learn about (*24, 25*). Children also work hard to learn to use words in writing (*17*).

One outcome of our research (this volume) has been the development of a set of pedagogical strategies by which children may be led to study words in a variety of different ways. The basic method we follow is that of a concept development task— a word sort activity. In this procedure, while children are studying words individually, they are always dealing with words in the context of a concept, be it phonological, syntactical, or morphological. We always work with words children know, i.e., words they can name or identify. Our object is that children now learn more about these words. No particular thing learned is considered the final answer. It is assumed, instead, that one might progress for a lifetime in learning more about the words of our language.

While word sorts can be used in both a pedagogical and research setting in order to investigate meaning or semantic categories, metalinguistic categories, or syntactic categories (11, 24, 25, 26), this paper focuses upon word sorts for letter-sound relationships useful in spelling and phonics. Spelling includes the discovery of generalizations that operate in standard orthography and phonics is one of the ways children recognize words in reading. The steps involved in word sorts are outlined late in the paper. Some readers may wish to preview these steps before reading on. The reason for presenting the steps so late is that the emphasis of the paper is upon the rationale and assumptions in using word sorts.

Teachers who use word sorts should make several assumptions about children and about words. First, and primarily, they should assume that children actively attempt to make sense out of the world and make hypotheses and generalizations about the world. They must assume that these generalizations include knowledge and action concepts for words (5, 22).

Second, they must have assumptions about the best "scope-and-sequence" of instruction. They must assume that the only realistic scope-and-sequence chart is the chart internal to children, the scope-and-sequence that children usually are actively abstracting from their own linguistic environment. While the invented spelling studies in this volume and other language acquisition studies (6, 8, 9,) point to general patterns of development in word knowledge, all children learn different oral and written words and learn those words at different rates (21); they learn those words in different dialects (20) with different vocal apparatuses (16).

As part of their assumption about scope-and-sequence, teachers who use word sorts must also be aware of the sometimes detrimental impact of externally imposed scope-

and-sequences such as those prescribed in basal readers and spelling texts. Children who come to a clinic have usually been taught from a number of different external scope-and-sequence charts. Often the reading books, workbooks, grammar text, and spelling texts all have different sequences. The child needing clinical help often has been taught from even more books than the average child. Typically, book authors choose the key word or exemplar and also the presumed right and wrong answers for any orthographic or phonic pattern being taught. Thus, the children who come to a clinic usually have failed in a large number of these conflicting sequences. They have little confidence in their knowledge about how the letter-sound system works and little confidence in their ability to learn the system, even if initially their hypotheses were good. In response, these children often have shut down the internal scope-and-sequence progress so far as spelling-related tasks go.

The third thing that teachers who use word sorts must assume is that every person will have different members in any category and yet there will be shared members and a developmental progression toward "standard" or "adult" categories. This is a crucial assumption. For instance, I have a category for the word *bell*, the thing that used to ring to call school to order. I have a subcategory having to do with meaning. This subcategory contains the different meanings I assign to *bell* in different contexts. I can use *bell* in sentences and stories and I can usually understand what is meant when other people use *bell*; so I have a functional subcategory for *bell* (which can include metalingustic knowledges about words in general). I can even, when asked, assign *bell* to a category dear (or not-so-dear) to the hearts of reading teachers; I can put *bell* in a "short E" category. If I am pressed to communicate with children in a classroom where these terms are used, I will even say that *bell "is a short E word."*

I bring up the topic of *bell* and short E because I recently asked a child to tell me the vowel sound he heard in *bell*. He then illustrated my claim that our categories have different members. He knew what word I meant because we were looking at a picture of a bell and he told me its use. Then he answered my question firmly: "Long A," he said, "It rhymes with *tell*." I wasn't sure which word he meant: t-a-i-l, the thing a dog wags; or t-e-l-l, what you do with a story. Then he pointed to the word *tell*. When I asked him to use *tell/tail* in a sentence, he said: "You shouldn't tell on people."

I might not have been so impressed with this young man's confidence in his judgment had I not been equally certain at one time that *bell and tail* and *tell* were rhymes and that the last two sounded exactly alike. In my Alabama dialect, *bell* is a long vowel word. However, a workbook page corrected with a red pencil might convince the child that he really is dumb in phonics and in spelling. If reading is taught so that letter-sound relationships become too central and so that comprehension is ignored, the child might even believe that he is dumb in *reading*.

To illustrate the variability in category membership across age levels, Anderson (*1*) did an intriguing experiment using cups and glasses (*15*). While her experiment did not use words, it still has implications for word sorting techniques. She took 25 cups and glasses, all different. She asked children aged three, six, nine, and twelve to do four tasks: 1) name the items; 2) sort them into cups versus glasses (also put items they thought were neither cup nor glass into a leftover pile); 3) define *cup* and *glass*; and 4) choose the best exemplar for each category [a typicality rating (*18, 19, 2, 3*)].

Anderson found, as have Read (*17*), Henderson (*14*), and others, that children agree quite a bit; they make sense out of categories in their world in order to communicate. Across ages, however, the categories children made did not hold the same members; older children tended to put more items into the leftover pile. The definitions the children gave indicated they realized category boundaries are vague or fuzzy. The children tended to use explanations that indictated a particular vessel was "kindalike" a cup, but "people usually call it a glass." They used hedges to indicate distinctions within their categories. Another drinking vessel might be rejected completely and placed in the leftover pile. Children rejected instances from a category according to how they, as individuals, defined the category.

Anderson's work is another illustration that people do not all share the same members within any category, even if they use the same title for the category or concept (3). The young man I described used the title "long A words," but his long A category included *bell*, a word that would usually be wrong according to any phonics or spelling book answer key. Teachers are often aware, at least implicitly, of the vagueness or fuzziness of word categories in letter-sound relationships; they complain loudly about misleading pictures and questions in classroom games and on worksheets. Teachers often ask for a way of stressing sensible letter-sound relationships in a manner that makes sense to the internal scope-and-sequence of the individual child, yet which will lead to a match with adult conventional spelling and word recognition strategies.

Since I believe that young children beginning to read may not recognize that our word concept boundaries are vague, I have been exploring the use of word sort techniques with children. The purpose of the word sorts is fourfold: 1) to follow children's internal scope-and-sequence, 2) to lead toward "standard" generalizations about orthography and phonics, 3) to illustrate to children that they can differ from other people and yet be correct within their own defined standards, and 4) to capitalize on well-established learning principles coming from concept development research (7).

The word sorts used at the McGuffey Reading Center at the University of Virginia are very much like Anderson's cups and glasses sorts. Anderson's cups and glasses were well-known items in children's environment. Similarly, we use words that are already in children's reading vocabularies—words which have been made into sight vocabulary words, whether they came from a basal reader story, library book, language experience chart, cereal box, or from a request to compose an individual story/report.

We assume that generalizations are based upon the well-known rather than the partially-known and, certainly, should not be applied to the unknown. At the McGuffey Center, the children build word banks and thesauruses or wordbooks of these well-known words. Word banks are most easily used for the sorting task itself while the thesauruses and wordbooks are used to record the results of these sorts.

A teacher may guide a word sort for a beginning reader in a very structured manner; we have called these sorts

Structured Word Sorts (26). In the structured word sort, the teacher establishes the category to explore, such as *short vowel patterns* or *consonant digraphs*. Preferably, the child picks the exemplar (or prototype) word for the category. If not, the teacher attempts to pick the most central exemplar from the child's word bank. The teacher may pick *bread* and *meat* from the child's bank and ask for sortings under these two words according to vowel patterns. Then steps for sorting are used.

An important alternative to the Structured Word Sort is the *Open-Ended Word Sort.* Here, the teacher allows the child to suggest the categories and to range as widely into letter-sound relationships, etymological kinships, or semantic relationships as is wished. Obviously, either type of word sort may be used diagnostically as well as for instructional purposes.

In either form, the basic steps of a word sort are the following.

1. Decide, with the child, the categories to be sorted and make a place for "leftovers."

2. Let the child sort the word cards under the title or exemplar for each category; put leftovers in the leftover pile.

3. Redefine the category: have the child restate the pattern he is using for sorting.

4. Ask for reaffirmation of choices: ask the child to go down each list and tell you if each one fits the category (strength of decision).

5. Make some distinction between members that fit the category very well and those that are "fuzzy" yet do not quite belong in the leftover pile.

6. Ask for a redefinition of the rule or generalization. Now the child has a rule and clear members, clear nonmembers, and borderline cases distinguished from one another.

7. Optional, but very fruitful: Collect word sort lists in a personal wordbook or thesaurus. One convention for "fuzzy" words that we have used in wordbooks is to put borderline cases in parentheses. Often a child will decide to remove a parenthesis and declare, *"Now* that word fits."

Why go to all this trouble? Because each person will have some different members in his/her category, we should have individual collections rather than all working on a common exercise like those found in typical workbooks. Also, the child is working from well-processed units, known words rather than perhaps-known words. In workbooks, much time is spent working not with written words, but with pictures used to represent a word category. We want any word category children work with to be tied to actual words a child has used and will use in reading.

More than that, by using word sort tasks such as we have outlined, we have made the children the judges and monitors of their categories. We build in demands for autonomy. We have also built the basis for helping children decide, personally, what is worth remembering. This places responsibility on the children, but responsibility that the children are capable of assuming.

While we would be delighted to think we had discovered a natural scope-and-sequence, I think there is some strong evidence of a natural pattern of development which we can explore in word sorts. At the same time, children have been taught by various approaches and have learned quite different things. We attempt to follow the pattern of development which occurs in the evolution of children's spellings (see chapters by Henderson and Beers) as much as possible because we think it gives us a general framework; however, at all times we follow the scope-and-sequence that we find with the children. We also have to look at the effects of classroom teaching upon the children's natural development. I'll give an example of the interaction between classroom instruction and a child's natural development and how they work in word sorts.

Recently, one child in the clinic went through five different word sorts before she produced the one I knew she was capable of doing and needed to do. Yet, along the way, she revealed a wealth of word knowledge; her concept of how words work began to branch widely.

The teacher had set up a number of language exploration centers in the classroom. The child had worked through a consonant center in which she sorted pictures of things whose names began with a variety of single consonant and consonant digraph sounds. She had also collected a number of sight vocabulary words beginning with the letter t- including some words beginning with th-. I asked her to sort some of her cards by beginning letters. She had never before sorted by two letters at the beginning of words.

She started by making a sort which included these words:

top
Tom
turkey
the
turtle
they

I asked her to think how these words were alike. She answered that they all began with the letter *t-*. I wrote the words in a list and asked her to draw a line under the letter *t-* at the beginning of each word. THAT was the concept she described to me and she was exactly accurate. The words do begin with the letter *t-* and I was able to praise her; furthermore, she was aware that the praise was sincere because she set the category and checked the category on her own terms.

She did not, however, give me the concept I had in mind and that the consonant center she had worked on in her classroom was designed to help her develop. I think this was a crucial point. She had declared a valid category or concept for her words and she had picked examples that fit the category consistently. I could leave it there if that were as far as I thought she could go at the time, but she demonstrated readiness for the letter-sound associations for *t-* and *th-* by doing the other steps in the center in her classroom. So, as a teacher, I had to decide how to praise her for the concept she illustrated while still encouraging her to try the concept I had in mind and that I thought would be helpful for her.

One of the four purposes of using word sorts is to allow youngsters the realization that words *may* be categorized in many different ways. So I asked this child to recopy her letter *t-* list in her wordbook; then I asked her to look at the word cards again to see if there were other ways she could sort them. This time she found the three-letter words: *top, Tom, the*. Again, she had a valid category with examples that fit her category. This time she also had clear nonmembers: *turkey, they*. The category was still not what I wanted, but we labeled it "three-letter words" in the wordbook and went on to yet another sorting. She finally had five lists including the *t*- versus *th*-distinction I had pressed her for: letter *t*- words, three-letter words, living things, *t*- sound words, and *th*- sound words. The titles might offend a purist, but they came primarily from the child and reveal much about her growing conception for how words work.

This child's sorts met all of the four purposes for word sorts. They followed her internal scope-and-sequence, yet they *moved toward* standard orthographic generalizations (*20*). The sorting technique allowed her to differ from other children in her classroom. It gave her the chance to have a clearly stated, understandable rule or generalization with members and nonmembers clearly distinguished (*7*). The rules and members, however, came from her developing knowledge.

It is the ability to look at words in many ways—in stable, memorable ways—that interests us in word sorts. Children use the less useful categories less frequently and the more useful categories more often. This young lady soon decided that "three-letter words" was not a very useful category for her. She quickly had too many useless words tied to the category, so she decided to take those pages out of her wordbook. The category did not help her remember anything she wanted to remember and it did not help her predict anything useful about new words.

As children become more adept at working with words and begin to read more widely, we encourage them not just to sort old words, but to actively seek out new words for their categories. We call these seeking activities *word hunts*. We use word hunts when children have a good grasp on the categories they are currently using and are seeking to expand their vocabularies. They may hunt for words which have certain prefixes or suffixes; they may look for nouns or verbs; they may look for words that fit a semantic category. In any case, we still ask the child to "define" the category:

> *What are you looking for?*

We ask for a statement of the criterion used:

> *Why did you pick this word for this category?*

We ask for strength of decision:

> *Does it fit?*

I have become increasingly impressed with this approach when I have heard a student say; "Well, you know, this word seems like it could be a noun—then again, it seems like it could be a verb." Or "This word just almost seems like it would fit, but it doesn't for me." These children seem to be saying, along with Anderson, that they understand category boundaries are vague when you take a close look at them.

Anderson speaks of boundaries as being "fuzzy," but we might cast this important insight into a more positive light by saying that boundaries are "alive." Whatever her metaphor, her cup and glass research is as intriguing as the children's word sorts. We might claim that the wisest people in any field are those who, while making use of central tendencies or invariance, also are strongly aware of the vagueness or aliveness of boundaries, categories, or definitions (27). The lesson I draw is that we must observe and explore children's concepts for words with them and allow the children to share our delight in their living boundaries. I believe that, in this manner, we will not divorce word exploration from other meaningful exploration in reading and language.

References

1. Anderson, E.S. "Cups and Glasses: Learning that Boundaries Are Vague," *Journal of Child Language*, 2 (1975), 79-103.
2. Anglin, J.M. *The Growth of Word Meaning*. Cambridge, Massachusetts: MIT Press, 1970.
3. Anglin, J.M. *Word, Object, and Conceptual Development*. New York: W.W. Norton, 1977.
4. Bates, E. *Language and Context: The Acquisition of Pragmatics*. New York: Academic Press, 1976.
5. Beers, J.W., and E.H. Henderson. "A Study of Developing Orthographic Concepts among First Graders," *Research in the Teaching of English*, 11 (1977), 133-148.
6. Brown, R. *A First Language: The Early Stages*. Cambridge, Massachusetts: Harvard University Press, 1973.
7. Bruner, J.S., J. Goodnow, and G. Austin. *A Study of Thinking*. New York: John Wiley & Sons, 1956.
8. Clark, H.H., and E.V. Clark. *Psychology and Language: An Introduction to Psycholinguistics*. New York: Harcourt Brace Jovanovich, 1977.
9. deVilliers, P.A., and J.G. deVilliers. *Early Language*. Cambridge, Massachusetts: Harvard University Press, 1979.
10. Estes, T.H. "Reading, Language Comprehension, and Knowledge of the World," paper presented at the Twenty-Second Annual Convention of the International Reading Association, Miami Beach, Florida, 1977.
11. Gillet, J.W., and M.J. Kita. "Words, Kids, and Categories," *Reading Teacher*, 32 (1979), 538-542.

12. Goodman, Y., and C. Burke. *Reading Strategies: Focus on Comprehension.* New York: Holt, Rinehart and Winston, in press.
13. Harste, J.C., and C.L. Burke. "A New Hypothesis for Reading Teacher Research: Both Teaching and Learning of Reading Are Theoretically Based," in P.D. Pearson (Ed.), *Reading: Theory, Research, and Practice,* Twenty-Sixth Yearbook of the National Reading Conference. Minneapolis, Minnesota: Mason Publishing, 1977, 32-40.
14. Henderson, E.H. "Developmental and Cognitive Aspects of Learning to Spell with Implications for Teaching and Diagnosis," presented at the Twenty-Second Annual Convention of the International Reading Association, Miami Beach, Florida, 1977.
15. Labov, W. "The Boundaries of Words and Their Meanings," in C.J. Bailey and R. Shuy (Eds.), *New Ways of Analyzing Variations in English.* Washington, D.C.: Georgetown University Press, 1973.
16. Lieberman, P. *On the Origins of Language.* New York: Macmillan, 1975.
17. Read, C. *Children's Categorization of Speech Sounds in English.* Urbana, Illinois: National Council of Teachers of English, 1975.
18. Rosch, E. "Cognitive Reference Point," *Cognitive Psychology,* 7 (1975), 532-547.
19. Rosch, E. "Cognitive Representations of Semantic Categories," *Journal of Experimental Psychology,* 104 (1975), 192-223.
20. Smith, E.B., K.S. Goodman, and R. Meredith. *Language and Thinking in School,* Second Edition. New York: Holt, Rinehart and Winston, 1976.
21. Spache, G., and E. Spache. *Reading in the Elementary School,* Fourth Edition. Boston: Allyn and Bacon, 1977.
22. Stauffer, R.G. *Directing the Reading-Thinking Process.* New York: Harper and Row, 1975.
23. Stauffer, R.G. *The Language Experience Approach to the Teaching of Reading.* New York: Harper and Row, 1970.
24. Sulzby, E. "Children's Explanation of Word Similarities in Relation to Word Knownness," in P.D. Pearson and J. Hansen (Eds.), *Reading: Disciplined Inquiry in Process and Practice.* Clemson, South Carolina: National Reading Conference, 1978.
25. Sulzby, E. "Semantic Salience in Relation to Word Knownness," paper presented at the Twenty-Eighth Annual Meeting of the National Reading Conference, St. Petersburg, Florida, 1978.
26. Tucker, E. Sulzby. "Word Concept Development Activities," paper presented at the Twenty-Second Annual Convention of the International Reading Association, Miami Beach, Florida, 1977.
27. Wittgenstein, L. *Philosophical Investigations,* Third Edition. New York: Macmillan, 1958.

Chapter Twelve

Word Knowledge and Reading Disability
Edmund H. Henderson
University of Virginia

One important outcome of our study of children's developing concept of word has been the sharper focus these stages provide in the diagnosis of language learning disabilities. In a manner similar to that of Goodman's "miscues" in reading, errors in spelling may now be categorized as 1) predictable and indicative of a particular stage of development or 2) deviant and indicative of some incapacity or misconstruction. In each case, the general stage of development and the characteristics of the deviations are suggestive of the kind of experience, including specific word-concept development that might be thought appropriate to correct and advance the pupils' understanding of English spelling.

Before illustrating these procedures concretely, it may be helpful to consider, first in general terms, some of the relationships between spelling and writing and spelling errors and reading miscues. Spelling errors and word identification errors are certainly related, but they are by no means mirror images. Obviously, it is possible to miscall a word either in isolation or in context and yet be able to spell it correctly. Words can be learned by a simple serial association of letters and they often are so learned, particularly in the early grades.

Words may be known almost automatically so they flow without thought from the pen and, so too, word elements may combine in "chunks" quite readily. Mnemonic devices, rules, jingles, the capital A in sepArate, may also help to guide the spelling right.

In reading, on the other hand, a great deal more is at play, much of it facilitative of correct identification and some predictive of miscues. Sense of text and internalization of style clearly afford phrase identification that is cued only minimally by discrete orthographic elements. The fluent reader does not examine words linearly and it is for this reason that Smith (8) has argued (and I think correctly) that fluent reading per se has little facilitative effect upon learning to spell. When, however, the reader's set for meaning overreaches the "given" or when his/her particular dialect predicts a different ordering of syntax, miscues may result for "known" words and may or may not do violence to the text as written. Thus, the correlation between spelling and word identification cannot be one to one, nor can any spelling system be learned unless words themselves are examined.

It must stand, nonetheless, that one indispensable element of word identification *is* orthographic knowledge, and it is largely absent in the early phases of learning to read. Memory of the text, anticipation of meaning, and a sense of the probable flow of written English may buoy the beginner; indeed, I believe this support is absolutely necessary for success. Yet words themselves must be learned and must gradually become indentifiable in their own right by minimal cues if a sufficient sight vocabulary is ever to be attained. Control of the vast low frequency lexicon, either for reading or for spelling, must depend upon this kind of conceptual mastery. For this reason, in the beginning there will be a very powerful relationship between word knowledge and word recognition, and advancement toward fluency as a reader will depend crucially upon smooth and progressive differentiation of this initial orthographic knowledge.

The function words of our language are by necessity high in frequency and powerfully supported for recognition by syntax (provided, of course, that they are presented in text and not isolated on flashcards). In phonetic terms, these words are highly irregular, and many are configuratively similar. Were it not for the powerful effects of frequency, they would be troublesome to learn. These are, moreover, the words most often confused by children who are failing. Lower frequency words are more regular phonetically and are most strongly supported by meaning. When children are allowed to make a beginning in natural text, their initial sight vocabulary will be found to contain about 50 percent high frequency words. The remaining 50 percent will spread across the lower frequency bands (5). It is through the examination of this latter class of words that a conceptual differentiation of orthographic knowledge may be gradually attained. It is for this reason that I strongly oppose controlled vocabularies for beginners. The high frequency words (the Dolch list, for example) lack the data from which word knowledge may be extracted; pattern controlled words (FAT, CAT, MAT), on the other hand, lack the diversity necessary for effective conceptual development (4).

My concern for phonetic regularity may seem surprising since our studies have tended to support the Chomskian model of phonological knowledge in terms of which English spelling is found nearly optimal in form. I believe it to be so; for the beginner, however, it clearly is not. One central finding by Read (7), replicated many times (2, 3), is that the beginning reader commences with a theory of orthography which though abstract is, nonetheless, heavily weighted with a direct phonetic letter-sound matching strategy. In a sense, children at this stage are "super-phoneticians." What they discern in the phonetic sequence of spoken words is quite free of higher level "orthographic overlay," and so they proceed to construct each word by setting out each named letter to its sound. They are consistent in this but not rigid. When letter names do not suffice or seem unnecessary, children substitute or omit elements. This remarkable adaptiveness attests their tacit sense that writing represents, but does not copy, speech. Progress in children's concepts of orthography must move *away from* rather than *toward* strict phoneme-grapheme correspondence. Our studies suggest that this comes about as children successively internalize surface pattern consistencies—specifically, the familiar vowel patterns, the patterns of affixation that flow with these, the stability of simple meaning elements across sound change. Further on, children enlarge these expectancies to include the somewhat different invariances found in polysyllabic forms and, ultimately, toward that point at which form-class or derivational units are differentiated by their internal regularities. Throughout, it is a progress from something like but distinct from a code, to a highly abstract relational representation of speech in visual form.

Is it any wonder I distrust those pedagogical programs that teach synthetic encoding—that insist to the children that they should stay where they are at the beginning—simply matching letters to sounds? Children who heed this advice will never advance. Little better are those programs that follow the analytic route implying that truth ends in the "discovery" that the e makes the vowel "say" its name. The pattern is valid, but it is merely a way station toward a far more complex and powerful set of relations. What may be said of teaching programs that imply that words are pictures to be learned as wholes and "bad" irregular spelling can only be achieved by recitation? My conclusion is that our well-intentioned conceits designed to "trick" children into learning to read are uniformly bad. We have underestimated children's capacities to deal with written language, and we have misunderstood the power and apprehensibility of written language in its diverse forms. Even the Chinese character is not a picture. What is needed for learning to read is support in natural language, abundant reading and writing, and a guided opportunity to differentiate that most remarkable of all graphic events, the written word.

Now let me turn to diagnosis and show what children's spelling can tell about their state of word knowledge. To provide a baseline, let me advance a set of spellings progressively as they might be rendered by normally developing children at successive stages. In each case you should conceive that the writer does not know the correct spelling by some primary means, sight recall or serial learning. He has simply "invented" it, constructed it as a best guess on the basis of what he knows (much of which is tacit knowledge) about words.

	Preliterate Prephonetic	Preliterate Phonetic	Letter Name	Vowel/ Transition
dog	ᶸᶸᶸ	D or DJ	DIJ	DOG
candy	scɵz]	K or KDE	KADE	CANDE or CANDY
bit	ɟN°c	B or BT	BET	BIT
Cinderella	kqwˤɭz43	S	SEDRLI	CINDARILA
went	—	—	WAT	WENT
table	—	—	TABL	TABEL or TIEBLE
bitter	—	—	BEDR	BITER
bake	—	—	BAK	BAIK

It is important to understand that the invented spellings here are not *absolutes*. They are possible examples that fit general strategic rules. They will vary from time to time, word to word, and dialect to dialect. Examination of a child's free rendering of a list of words—as with an old-fashioned spelling inventory—will allow one to discern a general categorical fit. The characteristics of these four categories may be described as follows.

Preliterate prephonetic. These are the typical and altogether normal productions of preschoolers who do not yet know in any stable, objective way what words are. Children have a notion about what writing is—that it isn't pictures, for example—and they have begun to inquire about letters. Perhaps they can print their name. When asked to spell/write words, they will cheerfully scribble or set down letter and letter-like symbols, including numbers and invented forms from left to right or right to left and often in a jumble.

Preliterate phonetic. This stage is characteristic of late kindergarten and beginning first grade. The principal feature is that these children have the idea that letter names stand for the elements of words. However, they know but a few words by sight and the concept of word as a stable object is still fragile and illusive. The salient beginning element is almost always captured and set down, but the rest escapes them. In short words, some other elements may be rendered but not in a long word like *Cinderella*. But the children know what letters do and so now they will not "fake" it with the look-like inventions used before.

Letter-name strategy. This stage emerges in mid-first grade or whenever knowledge of word is objectified and a stable initial sight vocabulary has been acquired. Known words are spelled correctly, but inventions take this character-istic form. If the phoneme is matched to a letter name, that letter appears in its appointed place in the word. If the phoneme does not have a matching letter name, as with the short vowels, the vowel which is "nearest" in the child's judgment is substituted. If there is no vowel, as with the vocalic consonants in TAB*LE* and BIT*TER*, the consonant serves alone. If the consonant is "predictable," as with the precon-sonantal nasal WE*N*T, it is omitted. Detailed accountings of this stage are given in Read (7) and Beers and Henderson (3), but the general flavor of the strategem suffices for a reasonable reliable recognition of what the child is doing.

Vowel transition. This stage is typically reached toward the end of grade one or the beginning of grade two, and it marks a powerful forward step in vocabulary acquisition. Under the imprint of a letter-name strategy, English words are bewilder-ingly homographic. In this new stage, however, children surrender their notions of short vowel substitution and accept the tense-lax pairings of post-vowel-shift English. Hence forward short vowels are spelled correctly. At the same time long vowels, which earlier stood alone, now begin to appear with a vowel marker though often with an incorrect one.

Beyond this point, stages of development range upward; but hereafter the demarkations, stage by stage, are far less firm. Errors of consonant doubling and the management of affixation in general are prominent in grades two and three. The stabilization of these regularities appears to await a fairly firm control of the common vowel patterns—sail/sale, feat/feet, lone/loan, and site/sight. The stability of the past tense morpheme *-ed* across sound changes tends to be realized in grade two, and some understanding of root constancy probably accompanies the learning of the base vowel patterns. Yet it is not uncommon in grade four to see *sail* spelled correctly but *sailor* spelled *salor* or *saler*. With the growing use of a larger, and mostly polysyllabic, vocabulary in grade four and beyond, the constancies of vowel patterns must be enlarged and differentiated in relation to stress and meaning, all of which may prepare the teenager to accommodate to those constancies of a new and abstract vocabulary as found in terms like *osmosis/ osmotic, capacious/ capacity, mnemonic/ amnesia.*

It is against this background of predictable developmental errors in spelling that we may now examine errors that are deviant and from these make speculations about how a disabled learner is dealing with written language. The administration of a spelling inventory provides us with essentially three kinds of information. First, we have a raw score for correctness, level by level. This is a power score and shows simply the degree to which correct production has been mastered. The diagnostician is interested in whether mastery comports with age, experience, and general intellectual capacity and whether unfamiliar words are attempted or omitted. Second, we examine the spelling errors themselves; and here we are able to establish a rough qualitative level in terms of our developmental stages. Finally, we concentrate upon any errors that deviate from the predicted pattern for any particular stage.

This analysis can be illustrated in the performance of two third graders, a boy and a girl, whom we screened for summer school instruction. Margie scored 95 percent on list one, 70 percent on list two, and 50 percent on list three. By the Betts criteria she would be termed instructional at grade two, achieving about one year below grade level, a state of affairs not at all in keeping with her better-than-average capacity and reasonably stable school experience. Examination of her spelling errors showed an almost perfect letter-name strategy. The vowels *e* and *a* were consistently substituted for short *i* and short *e*, respectively. Long vowels were unmarked. There was one deviant error in list one. *Blue* was *Bleu* which might be thought a reversal, but I suspect it reflects a sort of "blind" attempt to remember the letters. Another interesting error in list three was the spelling for *winter* which she rendered *wert*. Diagnosticians unacquainted with letter-name spelling would consider such a production hopelessly confused but, of course, it is not. If we forgive her reversal of the letters *r* and *t*, a not uncommon thing to do when one tries too hard, we can assume she intended *wetr*. Here, then, we see the predicted substitution of *E* for short *i*, the omission of the preconsonantal nasal *n*, the correctly rendered *T*, and the predictable vowel omission with the vocalic consonant *R*. But for the reversal, a perfect letter-name rendering.

Our qualitative analysis of Margie's spelling shows us a child who has pressed, on the power dimension, up to a mid-second grade level while operating conceptually at a middle first grade level. We could conclude that she is an attentive and diligent little student which, indeed, proved to be the case. We could also predict that, unless she made some advancement conceptually, she was headed for trouble, for power alone will not suffice for vocabulary acquisition.

In her summer program, Margie was given daily reading and writing activities and also began a daily word study sorting known words by their common short vowel patterns. This was done first on an auditory basis with pictures, then with sight words on small cards, and finally with open "hunts" for words she knew that fit the target patterns. When Margie could do these simple and very basic categorization tasks correctly and fluently, we began using the same general word sort and word hunt technique, with the common long vowel patterns. During the six week period of study, her creative writing began to show the telltale signs of an emerging transitional pattern.

Our second case, a little boy named Arthur, was, like Margie, functioning qualitatively at a letter-name level; but his profile was markedly deficient in several ways. In terms of power he was far lower, scoring 60 percent at level one and 30 percent at level two. Clearly, he had not been a diligent "plugger," for he knew no more on a memory basis than do most normally developing children at that stage of word knowledge. Unlike Margie, many of his errors were clearly deviant, two of these in rather interesting ways. Consider the words *was* and *of*. The most likely letter-name spellings of these would be *wos* and *ov* or *of*. Arthur spelled *was, wuz* and *of, uf*. Curiously, young children attune to the *s-z* variations quite easily (7). Arthur had abandoned it. Someone had been teaching him "his sounds." The second kind of deviant error, occurring largely in list one with words he believed he ought to know, was a sort of random throwing of letters in order to make "a word." *Where, weher; want, what; Mother, mudre's; things, tsigr.* One can see that the initial consonant does tend to be honored with here and there a "phonic" match—the *u* in *mother* as in *was* and *of*. But note that Arthur is doing something different from either the preliterate-prephonetic speller, who throws letter forms about with gay abandon, or the preliterate-phonetic speller who staunchly refuses to "fake" it. Arthur does fake it. It is as if, unable to remember just how things are and disillusioned with his own inner sense of how they might be, he has accepted such bits and pieces of "magic" as he has found in the classroom and applied these tensely and willy-nilly to the making of words. Indeed, our evidence that he did have some inner sense of word did not reveal itself until the latter part of list two when he was encouraged to and apparently did make unself-conscious "attempts."

Arthur's circumstance was thus very different from Margie's. Conceptually they were about on a par, but Margie's knowledge was functional; Arthur's was not. Our plans for this lad differed accordingly. First, we undertook to involve him intellectually in projects and activities around which and for which language played a part. He listened to accounts read to him and others on records and tapes. We tried conscientiously to "fill him" with sound, purposeful language. We used every device we could think of to support him in the "reading" of text—real stories; pattern stories; jingles; songs (with guitar and drum); and the "work horse" resource, his own dictation. From this immersion, his initial sight vocabulary began to stabilize and the frantic confusion with *what, where, when, went, want* and *these, them, they, then*—the Dolch list look-alikes—began to abate.

For word study, we gave Arthur sorting tasks using pictures and sight words that ran the gamut from meaning and syntax to initial consonant and cluster. We would make a grouping of pictures and have him guess the category, then do the same with words (always words we *knew* he could identify at sight). We would have him do the same and make us guess the category he had chosen. These activities were short, breezy, informal and, whenever possible, included other youngsters. Our objective was to break down his belief in "magic" and reawaken his curiosity and confidence in examining that marvelous thing called a word. Toward the end of the six-week session, Arthur began to pursue some of the more formalized tasks with which Margie had begun. Both children progressed; neither one was yet at grade level or intellectual level, much less a mature and fluent reader. They were, however, still just eight years old and there was time if the curriculum would afford it to them.

One final anecdote will conclude this essay which has been designed to give some flavor and sense of those insights that our studies of word knowledge seem to provide. Frederick, aged fifteen, performed far better on a spelling inventory than our two third graders, but by no means so well as he should. As I recall, his scores were 100 percent at fourth and fifth grade levels; but at sixth, seventh, eighth, and ninth grade levels, his scores wavered around 60 percent. High frequency words were letter perfect. Basic vowel patterns were flawless. Errors commenced with such demons as *separate* and *occurring* but more conspicuously with words like *finally* spelled *finly* and *financially* spelled *finantialy*.

Here was a lad who had been an "A" student in his elementary years, but who had dozed through the following years. His basic knowledge of English word form was sound, but he simply had not carried things forward to the grand lexicon of adulthood. A day later, without showing him the corrected copy of his spellings, I asked Frederick to spell *final*. He did so correctly. Then *finally*. Again, he spelled it right. Next I said, "Spell *dance*." He did so. "Spell *finance*; spell *financial*; spell *financially*." All three were spelled correctly! Was this some miracle? Not at all. The invariance of root propelled him to correctness; he was unaware of it, but I think one need not be. When I asked him why *financially* was spelled with a *c*, he replied that English was crazy that way! I then asked him to spell *initial* and *initially*, both of which he rendered correctly.

If he had studied a little Latin and Greek, Frederick probably would have gotten a handle on these things quite readily. I have often heard others say *that* is how they learned to spell. But it seems to me that we might arrive at about the same place, even though we missed the pleasures of Gaul and the Rubicon. Frederick and a group of amazingly keen teenagers led my students and me on a wild chase of words for over a month. We wore out dictionaries, scrapped a good deal, laughed a lot, and often ran out of time to practice "study skills," "note taking," and the high art of "answering essay questions." The fact is that all of us learned more about words than we really needed to know. But Frederick and the others learned much about how to look at words in many dimensions; and, therein, I think lies the secret.

English spelling clearly is abstract, and so it must be if it is to fulfill its office in the language we speak. Chinese is more abstract; nonetheless, it is comprehensible to millions and gracefully translatable to our tongue. Spanish, under the care of the Reãl Academia Española, has enjoyed "a reformation" continuously for 200 years, to the end that scholarly dialect has been well-controlled and a fairly high degree of phonetic regularity has been achieved. Not surprisingly, spelling errors are relatively rare among Spanish speaking minors. Among young Spanish adults, however, correct spelling does pose a serious problem (1,6). And this problem may well arise as a consequence of the artificiality of that orthographic system (9). Tinker as we will, our "reforms" seem less fruitful than they might appear on the surface. I conclude that we should be more accepting of our written language as it is. Changes in it will doubtless come to pass, but language spoken and written is certainly organic at its base. No mechanistic coding will "correct" it. Pedagogically, this means that we must treat this "gift" more kindly. We must use it for the best purposes of thoughtful communication and project its use more naturally with youth.

References

1. Alanzo, Maria Rosa. *Apuntes do ortografia.* Merida, Venezuela: *Universidad di los Andes*, 1965.
2. Beers, J.W. "First and Second Grade Children's Developing Orthographic Concept of Tense and Lax Vowels," doctoral dissertation, University of Virginia, 1974. *Dissertation Abstracts International*, 35, 08-A, 4972. University Microfilms No. 75-04694.
3. Beers, J.W., and E.H. Henderson. "A Study of Developing Orthographic Concepts among First Grade Children," *Research in the Teaching of English*, Fall 1977, 133-148.
4. Gibson, E., and H. Levin. *The Psychology of Reading.* Cambridge, Massachusetts: MIT Press, 1975.
5. Henderson, E.H., T.H. Estes, and S. Stonecash. "An Exploratory Study of Word Acquisition among First Graders at Midyear in a Language Experience Approach," *Journal of Reading Behavior*, 4, 3 (Summer 1972), 21-30.
6. Marcos Marin, Francisco. *Liñguistica Y Lengua Española.* Madrid: Cincel, 1975.
7. Read, C. *Children's Categorization of Speech Sounds in English.* Urbana, Illinois: National Council of Teachers of English, 1975.
8. Smith, Frank. *Psycholinguistics and Reading.* New York: Holt, Rinehart and Winston, 1973.
9. Temple, Charles. "An Analysis of Spelling Errors in Spanish," doctoral dissertation, University of Virginia, 1978.